THE LIFE GUIDE YOU ACTUALLY NEED

REAL SKILLS, REAL TALK, REAL TOOLS FOR YOUNG ADULTS FIGURING IT OUT

LISA PIATETSKY

Disclaimer

This book offers insights, ideas, and real-world guidance based on the author's own research, experiences, and perspective. It's meant to inform and inspire—not to replace professional advice.

If you're facing a personal challenge—health-related, legal, financial, or otherwise—please reach out to a qualified professional. Everyone's situation is different, and trained experts can help you figure out what's right for you.

The author and publisher cannot take responsibility for how the information is used, but we hope it empowers you to make thoughtful, informed choices. Thank you to Brian Skillen (and team) at PublishingHackers.com for their much appreciated direction and support.

The Life Guide You Actually Need: Real Skills, Real Talk, Real Tools: For Young Adults Figuring It Out

Copyright © 2025 by Lisa Piatetsky

Published by Rollostan Press.

All rights reserved. No part of this book may be used or reproduced in any manner whatsoever without written permission except as allowed by U.S copyright law.

Printed in the United States of America

First Edition

ISBN 978-0-9748473-1-3 (Paperback)
ISBN 978-0-9748473-2-0 (Ebook)

Contact Lisa Piatetsky at L.Piatetsky.Author@Gmail.com

Dedication

To my son, Porter,
a beautiful soul with a future full of promise,
a thoughtful young man whose humor brought smiles to many,
whose absence is felt in the quiet moments.

He left us too soon, but his spirit lives on in every word,
in every hope I have for those who are still finding their path.

And to you, dear reader: May this book be a beam, lighting
your journey, a reminder that your life holds meaning. It is
never too early or too late to develop into who you want to be.

Table of Contents

Preface
Why Now? The Need for Support and Direction — ix

Chapter 1
Getting Started — 1

Chapter 2
Finding Your Best Living Situation: From Locations to Roommates — 5

    Location — 6
    Roommates — 7

Chapter 3
Romantic Relationships — 11

    The Language of Love — 12
    A Good Starting Point — 12
    Developing Good Communication Skills — 13
    Long-Distance Relationships — 14
    Online Dating — 15

Chapter 4
Finances — 17

    Bank Accounts — 18
    Credit Scores and Debt — 19
    Investment Accounts — 20
    Purchasing Auto Insurance — 27

Chapter 5
Caring for Your Health: Physical and Mental Well-Being — 31

    Medical Insurance — 32
    Lowest Monthly Premium — 33
    Moderate Monthly Premiums — 33
    High Monthly Premiums — 34
    Terminology for Health Care Plans — 34
    Government Run Medical Insurance — 36
    The Importance of Seeking Health Care — 37
    Mental Health — 38

Chapter 6
Living a Healthy Life — 43

    The Importance of Sleep — 46
    Healthy Eating for Your Future — 48
    Recipes — 56
    Exercise for Your Health — 66

Chapter 7
Relationships With Family — 69

Chapter 8
Seeing the World — 73

    Traveling Abroad — 75
    How to Start Traveling — 76

Chapter 9
Creativity — 81

    So How Do You Become Creative? — 83
    Famous Creators Through the Centuries — 84
    Ending Thoughts About Creativity — 96

Chapter 10
Prioritizing for
Round-the-Clock Success   97

     Procrastination   98
     Goal Setting   100

Chapter 11
Government   105

     Executive Branch   106
     Legislative Branch   107
     Judicial Branch   107
     Checks and Balances   108
     The Popular Vote   108
     The Electoral College   109

Chapter 12
Politics   111

Chapter 13
Finding a Job   115

     Résumé   117
     Getting an Interview   118
     Mentors   119

Chapter 14
Business and Entrepreneurship   121

     Make It Work: Real Ways to Earn and Run a Business   125
     Money-Making Aspects of Business   125
     Learn These Important Aspects of Business   126

Chapter 15
Future Proofing for Personal Stability:
Mindsets for an Unpredictable World   127

    Technology   128
    COVID Pandemic   130
    Climate Change   131
    Politics   132
    Education   132
    Social Shifts   133
    Social Media   134
    Things You Can Do to Adapt to Change   134
    Critical Thinking   135
    Other Ways to Have a Full Life During Difficult Times   136

Chapter 16
The End is The Beginning   139

Resources   141

    Food   141
    The Body, Health, Mental Health, and Fitness   142
    Finances and Entrepreneurship   142
    Politics/Government   143
    Personal Growth   143
    Creativity   143

PREFACE

Why Now? The Need for Support and Direction

Dear Reader,

If you chose this book, you are likely in a stage of life when many things are changing. Whether you are eighteen or thirty, life can be difficult if you don't have some answers to important questions.

Maybe you are out on your own for the first time. Maybe you are in college, or you are starting a new job. You could be beginning or ending a relationship. You may have been on your own for a bit, wondering why no one told you how to navigate adulthood.

That's where this book comes in!

This is not a book of lectures, fluffy inspiration, or unrealistic lists with no real-life use. It is a handbook. A toolkit. A guide to help you navigate some of the most important, exciting, and at times, overwhelming aspects of life as a young adult.

Inside you will find real talk about:

- How to understand finances and avoid debt
- What you need to know about health and mental health, and how to find help when you need it
- How to stop procrastinating and set goals
- How to make sense of politics and government
- How to build lasting relationships, ignite your creativity, travel, deal with a changing world, and much more

This is not a book of advice. It's about learning to think for yourself, building habits that can support you through the rest of your life, and figuring out how to live well on your own terms.

Whether you are eighteen or thirty, whether you feel confident or feel lost, you are not the only one. Your life is a journey. It is not a test that needs answers right now. People grow—and they change. It's OK to try things out. It's okay, OK to fail and start again. If one path isn't a fit, it is perfectly fine to try something new.

The aim of this book is to walk with you through the hard things:

- Making mistakes
- Feeling confused
- Changing your mind

It also encourages you to feel good about proceeding forward, having successes and mastering your independence. As you move through these pages, you will gather new tools, ideas, and perspectives that will help you to take your next steps with confidence. Here, you will learn what is important to you as you proceed forward. Let this be a staring place, your opening chapter—not one that requires perfection but one that gives you permission to grow.

You've got this. You can prevail over adulthood.

CHAPTER 1
Getting Started

Coming into your own is often both confusing and stressful. It can also be exciting and exhilarating. Now that you are stepping into your independence and making decisions, wouldn't you feel better making decisions knowing how they could change and enhance your life? Just think of the possibilities. What would happen if you felt confident, knew how to handle finances, felt capable in social situations, developed satisfying relationships, and walked in social circles with others who shared your interests and world views?

I moved out of my parent's house at seventeen. It was an exciting time. I started college in a county an hour or so from where I grew up and loved the exposure to so many new ideas shared by my teachers. I made several new friends in the classes I was taking—mostly artists and musicians whose interests aligned with mine. I also had two roommates in a three-bedroom home. But this living situation quickly became a source of conflict.

When I started college, I had no idea how to assess whether I'd be compatible with my roommates. One girl was twenty with a full-time job; the other was twenty-two and was finishing up her BA. Looking back, it's no surprise we didn't match. My roommates wanted me to join them at bars and sports events, but since I was underage, drinking didn't interest me, and neither did their sports activities. The more times I declined to join my roomies, the more I could feel the tension building between us. Eventually, the situation became unbearable and depressing.

I realized I'd made a mistake in choosing this living situation, and I decided to take action. I found a couple of students looking for a roommate and moved in with them. They were in my age group, both starting out at college and living on their own for the first time. It was a fun situation where I felt accepted and safe. Had I known how to think through choosing roommates the first time, I likely would have made a better choice from the start.

This book is about helping you make those more-informed choices. Life is sometimes difficult for young adults, but in this book, you will learn practical ways to navigate the challenges ahead.

By equipping yourself with knowledge and skills, you will feel more at ease and set yourself up for success. This book is a guide to setting your course for the life you wish to have, setting you up to flourish and make decisions that secure your desired future. By reading this book, you'll jumpstart your growth by examining the following topics:

- Finding a job
- Choosing a mentor
- Finding health coverage
- Getting medical and mental health care
- Prioritizing social activities alongside school and work responsibilities
- The benefits of volunteering
- Locating housing
- Having successful romantic relationships
- Choosing roommates
- Understanding finances
- Living a healthy lifestyle
- Building your own identity through self-discovery
- And other relevant topics

This book will help you to navigate a path to master young adulthood.

Enjoy your journey!

CHAPTER 2

Finding Your Best Living Situation: From Locations to Roommates

Finding a comfortable living situation takes some thought. My favorite location as a young person was in a house with three or four roommates. We often ate together and went out together, becoming close friends. We also did our own thing. In fact, it seemed easy to have autonomy. We found comfort knowing home was safe and filled with people who cared about each other.

It had a garden which I enjoyed working in and was alongside a creek with blackberry vines. I enjoyed the twenty-minute bike ride to my college classes, when it wasn't raining. It was a fifteen-minute ride to the quaint downtown area. I was able to do my banking (before online banking was a thing). I stopped in at the café that served my favorites: croissants, pancakes, twenty varieties of tea, and bowls of oatmeal with fruit.

You may have a dream of what moving out on your own will look like. Let's say this dream looks something like a two-story condo in the heart of the city with your friend Jake or cousin Ellen. Now let's say your new job is forty minutes away—maybe sixty minutes during rush hour. You will have to figure out if there will be enough time to shower, dress, eat breakfast and walk your dog before you need to leave.

Location

When you are choosing an area, consider the grocery stores, gas stations, restaurants, gyms, and other amenities nearby. Does the area have what you need? Based on those criteria, decide whether the area has potential for you.

From there, make a list of what you are looking for in a living space:

- How many bedrooms and bathrooms do you need?
- Single dwelling, condo or apartment?

- What is the cost of living as the only occupant?
- What is the cost of sharing a space with roommates?
- Which situation can you afford?
- What are the crime statistics for the area? Contact the local police department's nonemergency line if needed.
- What do people who live in the area think about it?
- Are there assigned parking spots or on-street parking?
- What would your budget look like if you lived there? Consider utilities, food, gas, entertainment, and other necessities so you can decide whether you can afford the location you are considering.
- Are there special perks (community pool, hot tub, or clubhouse; fireplace, security monitoring; laundry room; in-residence washer and dryer; air conditioning; etc.)?

Roommates

If you can, hang out with potential roommates before you live together. While this is not always possible, it may help you understand whether a person is compatible with your lifestyle.

When picking a roommate, consider the following:

- Are they responsible and financially stable? Can they pay rent on time?
- Do they like to have people over to visit for a few hours, or do they want to have overnight guests? Will you want to have parties or dinner gatherings?
- Will they respect your things and your personal space (room, computer, and other items you purchased for personal use)?
- How will you handle food purchasing, cleaning supplies, and toilet paper? Will you each buy your own, or will you share?
- Are they willing to participate in cleaning? Are their habits similar to yours? How will you agree to maintain common areas?
- Will either of you have pets? How will you care for them?

- Do either of you participate in activities that might disturb the other at home? Are your schedules similar for sleeping, showering, playing music, and so on?

Finding a roommate is not an easy task. With due diligence, you can make a decent choice for both of you. Here are some ways to go about searching for a roommate:

- Ask friends or family members whether they know of anyone looking for a shared living situation.
- Check near colleges. Look for areas where you see ads for shared situations. Check the student housing office.
- Check listings at food co-ops, cafés, gyms, and restaurants.
- Ask Facebook friends (or other online groups) and post that you are looking for roommates.

Once you have found a place and a potential roommate, you will need your application accepted. Discuss beforehand whether you both have a decent credit rating.

Talk about how you will handle paying for bills (utilities, internet, and TV cable service). Your landlord may require both of you to have renter's insurance (see below).

Share ideas about furniture and how you will set things up and decorate. Talk about who has dishes, pots and pans, a vacuum, a mop, and other household essentials.

If there is not enough room for all of your belongings, you may be able to rent storage space on-site. Some buildings offer it for free with your rental. If there is a pet fee, the pet owner should pay for that.

Figure out how you will deal with the lease and cleaning deposit. You might discuss with the landlord or property manager if you can both pay individually for half of the rent each month and half of the deposit at the onset of renting.

Renter's insurance is always a good thing to look into. Some landlords require you to get it when signing a lease. Both of you would be responsible for your own policy. The insurance usually only covers the person named on the renter's coverage agreement.

Even though you may feel you don't need insurance, it's important to assess the cost of replacing your belongings. Losing a laptop, phone, clothes, furniture, video console, and TV would be costly to replace if a fire or theft occurred. The monthly fee for insurance is quite reasonable—about five dollars to twenty-five dollars a month. Some policies have a coverage limit. Be sure to shop around if one company doesn't fit your needs.

The cost of your policy depends on certain factors such as:

- How much your belongings are worth
- Whether you live in a higher-crime area
- Whether you live in the city
- Whether you pick a higher deductible rate (allowing you to pay a lower monthly premium)
- Whether your place has smoke alarms or a security system

Many times, you can bundle renter's insurance with your auto insurance. If you have both policies with the same company, they often can offer a discount.

Seach these sites for a good deal on coverage:

- www.lemonade.com
- www. nerdwallet.com
- www.policygenius.com

Becoming a roommate is the beginning of a different kind of relationship. Agree to be open and provide one another with a safe place to come home to. While not all roommates work out, many develop into a lifelong connection and become steadfast friends. Here's to new experiences and finding just the right roomie and place to live!

CHAPTER 3

Romantic Relationships

The Language of Love

From the initial flirtatious *hello* to becoming friends to having a committed relationship, there are so many aspects to developing a romantic relationship. One young man told me he met "the One" in the grocery store. She was holding a small watermelon, and he asked her how to tell if it was ripe. This interaction became the gateway to a conversation that lasted more than twenty minutes and led to them exchanging phone numbers. But was he right? Could she really be the One? Or was he just imagining what could be? How do relationships start? When do you know you are in love—and why do relationships end?

A Good Starting Point

Now that you are on your own and settled into a new living situation, you may be thinking about finding a companion. Perhaps you already have a special companion. Now is a good time to define what you are hoping for when forming a close connection.

Knowing oneself helps greatly when you are ready to select someone to get to know better. If you know who you are, you can better communicate what is essential to you. You can better imagine how a relationship fits into your life. How will you engage with another person while maintaining your own identity, allowing for self-exploration, and focusing on your goals?

You can take these steps to boost your self-awareness:

- Observe the feelings you have and actions you take. Do these aspects of yourself pull you down, or are they positive and give you strength? Get to know what you value.
- Ask yourself, When do you feel most like yourself? What type of people do you feel energized by or drained by?

- Explore your relationships with partners and friends. What patterns keep repeating. What needs have been met or unmet? Were there times when you compromised too little or too much?
- Identify relationships where you have felt understood and respected.
- Write a list of values that are important to you, such as independence, integrity, honesty, good listening, self-expression, patience, adventurousness, or curiosity. Identify your essential three values so you can avoid relationships that do not fit these criteria.
- Since relationships thrive when you have a strong sense of self outside of the relationship, try new things. Give yourself opportunities to expand.

As part of this self-exploration, consider how much time you have to give. How does work or school affect your availability? How will you fit in time with friends, visits with family, and other meaningful connections and activities?

Also think about what you expect from a relationship, keeping in mind what is reasonable within your situation. Strive to be supportive and flexible with one another. What type of commitment are you both willing to make? No one can be available all the time. There needs to be room for personal growth and doing activities that help you discover who you are. Will you both feel comfortable with taking "me" time?

Developing Good Communication Skills

Communication is key to any relationship, and developing these skills can take time. As you develop a bond, respect that you are both still individuals. You both should feel a level of comfort, trust, and understanding in expressing feelings.

Developing your ability to share about yourself, be vulnerable, and express emotions helps to build a sense of respect. Be sure to communicate your boundaries. For instance, you may wish to share that you want to continue to see friends, that you must take care of your dog on time, or that you are not ready for sexual relations. Be sure to discuss the limits and rules each of you find important to maintain.

A good sense of mutual respect is important to a healthy relationship.

Some warning signs that you are in a relationship that may not be healthy are:

- Not being listened to
- Being demeaned
- Being lied to
- Not being able to resolve conflicts respectfully or without yelling
- Experiencing violent or threatening behavior (This is not acceptable under any circumstances, and you must make sure you move from this situation, get help, and seek safety.)

These are not issues that should ever be ignored or tolerated.

Long-Distance Relationships

Living apart from your partner can be difficult and frequently brings on certain issues. If you are in a long-distance relationship, take steps to make it easier. Define how often and through which avenue you will communicate, such as:

- Texting
- Phone calls
- FaceTime
- Zoom
- Writing letters

Maintaining a romance from afar takes work, so be prepared to discuss:

- How you will communicate.
- How often you will see each other.
- When and where will you meet.
- What is agreed upon regarding your relationship. Decide whether you can see other people. Are you both committed, and what does that mean?

- How you will deal with feelings of jealousy, loneliness, and all the other possible emotions that may come up.

Online Dating

Online dating comes with its own challenges. Many people like the anonymity that meeting people on the internet affords. First examine why you are choosing to go online as opposed to meeting people in person—for example, through gatherings, volunteer opportunities (such as at animal shelters, political groups, neighborhood clean-ups), and other activities (such as seminars, book clubs, sports, or group meetings in your area).

Online encounters can be a way to build confidence while getting to know each other. It can also be a fun way to meet new people and discuss new ideas. But when moving from the friend zone to a more romantic relationship, be sure to protect yourself and take precautionary measures.

It's easy to assume that the people you speak to online are genuine about how they present themselves. This is where the danger lies when online dating. Without meeting the individual, you cannot be sure they are depicting themselves truthfully. Beware of the other person's reluctance to video chat, share photos, talk on the phone, or set up a time to meet. They may be a "catfish"—a predatory person who is not honest about their identity. They portray themselves as a totally different person to get something out of others: money, food delivery, or worse. They often have stories that just don't make sense. If you are feeling uncomfortable or suspect a person you met online is not being authentic, you should strongly consider removing yourself from the situation.

CHAPTER 4
Finances

Disclaimer: I am not a financial adviser, and I suggest you meet with someone at your bank to discuss investment opportunities.

Bank Accounts

I opened my first savings account in third grade, and we could make deposits at school on a weekly or monthly basis. It was like a bank club. The minimum deposit was fifty cents, and most of my friends put in one dollar per month.

There were no online banking opportunities and no debit cards then. You got your rather small envelope, which had a string to wrap around two heavy disks to seal it, and you would list the date and the deposit amount. Your name and account number were already printed on the front. By the end of the day, the envelope would come back to you with a red pencil mark by your deposited amount. If you wanted your money, you would have to go to the bank.

But all that has changed. Now you don't need cash or need to go into the bank. Electronic deposits from your employer and the convenience of online banking and transferring money to other accounts have made banking a breeze in all areas. You can even apply for a loan through your computer.

However you choose to do it, open a bank account. One of the most important reasons for doing so is to have control over your finances. You can learn how to spend money wisely and prepare for the future. Most banks have online spending charts to help you see how you spend your money (such as how much you spend on food, recreation, and clothes). This helps you take advantage of the power of saving, which not only gives you some security in case of an emergency, but also allows you to take advantage of certain opportunities. Paying attention to your finances also helps you focus on where you might cut back or, if you have extra, plan things like a road trip or an upcoming concert.

Also know that banks are a safe place for your money. Many banks in the United States offer insurance from the Federal Deposit Insurance Corporation (FDIC). You can insure up to $250,000 at each bank. This gives you assurance that money you've deposited in your bank will not be lost if the bank goes bankrupt or fails to operate for other reasons.

Credit Scores and Debt

Having a bank history also helps you begin to build your credit report. Lenders look to see if you can handle keeping a balance in your account without overdrafts. If your account requires you to maintain a minimum balance, you can further prove that you are not impulsive in your spending or have a frequent number of financial emergencies.

Having a bank account is a good way to get acquainted with bank staff, who can, in turn, help you when you are interested in getting a loan or a credit card. Having good credit can open many doors for you, such as obtaining a rental agreement for an apartment, a car rental, a car purchase, or even a job.

You can receive negative credit reviews by being late on payments. Unpaid payments such as utilities, rent, bank mortgages, car payments, and any other payment that becomes late not only can affect your credit but can also incur late fees, higher interest rates, and calls from collection companies. This is not a pleasant rabbit hole to go down.

Bad credit can interfere with getting loans, credit cards, getting utilities in your name, applying for an auto loan, renting a place to live, or buying a house. It can also harm an otherwise good set of references when applying for a job.

To ensure you have a good credit score, the best advice I can give you is to be sure you do not rack up debt. Only spend what you can pay comfortably monthly. The best way to do that is to make sure you do not miss credit card payments. Only spend what you can pay for monthly, and make paying your debt in full each month a goal. Keep in mind that credit is not free money. If you don't pay your minimum monthly payment, you can be charged interest as well as late fee.

Many people have a hard time with the burden of dealing with their debt. You can live debt-free by buying only what you can pay for at the moment of purchase. A savings account can help to handle emergencies and special purchases.

Depending on which account you choose, you can earn interest slowly or at a higher rate. You can usually open a basic bank account with under $100. Other types of accounts may require you keep a balance of anywhere between $500 (lower interest rate) to $5,000 (higher interest rate).

The amount you will earn in interest on accounts depends on the money you deposited into your savings account and the rate of yield. The interest you have on a yearly basis is called percentage yield. Compounded interest is the additional gains over time that your interest receives. Aim to find a bank with the highest interest-earning rates and no or low monthly fees.

Here are some of the types of accounts you may wish to consider:

- **Basic Checking Account.** You can use this type of account to handle your daily financial business, including writing checks, depositing money, making transactions with debit cards, online bill pay, and other amenities offered by your bank.
- **Interest-Bearing Checking Account.** This allows you to earn interest on your account balance but usually requires a minimum balance to be carried. Interest is gained when you invest your money into a bank account. Banks in turn use that money to make loans to others and investments for their own growth. In return, they pay you in interest.
- **Basic Savings Account.** It's easy to deposit into and withdrawal from these kinds of accounts. They can help you to save money while giving you interest on your balance.

Investment Accounts

Next, let's explore how you can increase your earnings through investing. Many banks have investment consultants who can help you understand and choose from multiple investment opportunities. Figuring out how you want to use and save your money is an important factor in what types of accounts you wish to have.

Some accounts allow you to gain daily, monthly, or yearly compounded interest. Compounded interest is calculated on the amount of initial investment and the interest you gain from your account's assigned interest (calculated either daily, monthly, or yearly).

Here is the formula to calculate compounded interest:

$$A = P(1 + r/n)^{nt}$$

A = final amount after interest
P = initial investment amount (principal)
r = annual interest rate
n = number of times interest is compounded per year
t = number of years you have held the account

Here is an example: A deposit of $3,000 at 5 percent annual percentage yield for ten years would be:

Daily Compounding	= $4,945.99*
Monthly Compounding	= $4,941.03
Yearly Compounding	= $4,886.68

*Because interest is paid out daily, it is possible to accrue more money at this interest level.

Certificates of Deposit (CDs)

These allow you to earn higher interest while your money is invested for a certain period. You can select a fixed term of one, three, or five years.

The annual percentage rate you will earn is available at the end of your term.

Always check with your bank or financial consultant to find out the current interest rate of return for your investment before deciding on a CD investment. Rates can vary in amount depending on the banks, brokerages, credit unions, and online services you review.

High Yield Savings Accounts

This type of account allows you to receive higher interest while keeping a higher minimum balance in your account. If the balance drops below this necessary amount, you will no longer be eligible to receive interest and may be asked to switch to an account that does not have these requirements.

Money Market Accounts

These accounts allow you to have both a savings and checking component with higher interest rates than standard accounts. They require you to keep a higher minimum balance.

Brokerage Accounts

These accounts are for buying and selling stocks, bonds, and mutual funds. They are overseen by expert fund managers who buy and sell investments for a group who contribute money to invest in an array of bonds, stocks, and securities.

Individual Retirement Accounts: IRAs and Roth IRAs

These types of accounts allow you to receive tax breaks while saving money for retirement. Which type you choose may have to do with your income at the time of starting the account and the projected income you will have when retiring.

- **IRA.** You may contribute your yearly amount tax-free (you won't get taxed for the money at the time of contribution). You will be taxed when you take it out at age 59 and 1/2 or later. If you take money out early, you will be charged a penalty rate of 10 percent.
- **Roth IRA.** These accounts are tax-free. The money is contributed after taxes are paid on your money. There are no tax deductions given on your yearly taxes. There are no taxes accrued on your earnings. You may withdraw the money you contributed at any time, at any age. The account must be at least five years old to take the earnings out.

FinTech (Financial Technology)

Fintech banking refers to tech-enhanced or digital-first banking. This type of service is provided away from a traditional bank or with bank affiliation. Their aim is to provide faster service, a user-friendly atmosphere, lower fees, quick transfers, budgeting and saving tools, credit building, and investment opportunities.

Some of fintech banking services are:

- **Peer-to-Peer Payments.** Send and receive money quickly (Venmo, Zelle, and Cash App).
- **Robo-Advisers.** These provide automated investment management (such as Betterment and Wealthfront).
- **Buy Now, Pay Later (BNPL).** Split payments into smaller amounts (such as with Klarna or Affirm).

Benefits of Fintech	Disadvantages of Fintech
Quick and easy sign-up	Potential data privacy risks
Lower fees	Limited customer service

Benefits of Fintech	**Disadvantages of Fintech**
Require no or low minimum balances	No branches with staff to meet with
No need to visit a bank	Not regulated like banks
Free educational tools	Some companies do not have FDIC protection
	Unclear fees, interest rates or usage terms
	Some apps encourage overspending

Bitcoin and Cryptocurrency

Disclaimer: Bitcoin is not my area of expertise. I advise you to read up on it and contact a financial adviser before you make investment decisions.

Is Bitcoin your thing? If you made an investment buying 100 bitcoins at the 2019 price of somewhere around $3,500 per bitcoin (an investment of $350,000), your bitcoins would now have a value of around $8,653,700 (selling for around $85,848.76 per bitcoin). Of course, most people don't have that amount of money to invest in Bitcoin. It is looked at as a less-stable investment. Just imagine if you bought 100 bitcoins when it was $1 per coin several years ago!

When I first heard of Bitcoin, I had no idea what it was. It seemed akin to Monopoly money. But when I dug deeper, I learned Bitcoin is the first decentralized cryptocurrency (currency not controlled by a bank or government). It was created in 2009 by an unidentified group going by the name of Satoshi Nakamoto.

The main goal behind Bitcoin was to create a digital currency that operated without the need for a central authority, such as a government or financial institutions. Bitcoin runs on a decentralized network of computers that verify and record transactions on a public ledger called the blockchain.

Bitcoin gained popularity over the years due to its potential to provide secure, transparent, and borderless transactions. It uses cryptographic techniques to ensure the integrity and security of transactions, making it difficult to duplicate or manipulate.

In the early days, Bitcoin faced skepticism and was primarily used by a small community of enthusiasts. People called it a commerce for the gaming crowd or techies, but it soon broke out of that narrow definition. It took hold and grabbed the interest of countries like the Central African Republic and El Salvador, which now use Bitcoin as their legal tender. Other countries have also welcomed Bitcoin for commerce. Many people recognized the possibilities allowed through purchasing Bitcoin, especially as its value began to rise. Bitcoin's independence from the limiting regulatory rules of financial institutions and governmental entities has broadened its appeal as an investment asset. Bitcoins are limited to 21 million coins, and many people who deal in bitcoins feel this limit makes it more valuable and rarer.

Altcoin

The term *altcoin* is used as the name for any other cryptocurrency. Altcoin often has faster blocktimes (speed of transfer), greater energy efficiency, and more anonymity compared to Bitcoin.

Altcoins typically are utility tokens for specific services. There are stablecoins, which are a more reliable value of exchange and less volatile. They are used more often in making international payments and they are used in decentralized financing.

Cryptocurrency Wallet

Similar to a digital wallet on your phone connected to a bank card, a cryptocurrency wallet stores, sends, and receives cryptocurrency. You use a private key to access your cryptocurrency. Always protect this code. Be sure to back it up in a safe manner. Treat it like a secret code. If you lose your code, it may be very difficult or impossible to recover. A public key is used for others to receive your funds. These keys work together.

There are several different kinds of wallets:

- **Hot Wallets (Online Wallets).** Managed through the internet on desktop or mobile apps. *Issues:* You must have security to protect against hackers.
- **Cold Wallets (Offline Wallets).** Managed offline for safer and more secure transactions. *Issues:* You need to be responsible for not losing your recovery code.
- **Hardware Wallet.** A device that stores your private key.
- **Custodial Wallet.** A wallet managed by a third party that holds your key.
- **Non-Custodial Wallets.** You hold control over your keys.

Investment Account Final Thoughts

Here are the biggest factors to explore before setting up an investing account:

- Are you interested in long-term or short-term investing?
- What will you be using this money for (emergencies, buying a car, retirement, etc.)?
- When do you need to access the money?
- If you are investing in the stock market, can you tolerate the ups and downs of this type of investment? Are there management fees? Do you want to stay away from certain investments? Do you care about if they support certain industries?
- Do you understand the tax issues involved with certain investments?

Consider the following:

- Find the type of investments that you feel most comfortable with.
- Start with small investments.
- Consider putting in a monthly amount.
- Consider a tax advantaged account like a Roth IRA or a 401(k).
- Keep up on interest rates offered, stock market opportunities, and its fluctuations.

I recommend that you start a retirement fund as early as possible. Time creeps up on you. I've watched relatives fail to plan, and the results were heartbreaking. Investing in interest-bearing accounts allows you to save as the interest grows through the years.

Another thing I recommend is learning about the stock market. If you understand how the market works, it likely will give you great indicators of where economics are headed, how certain sectors are doing, and the innovations that are present daily. I learned from watching a program on TV called *Power Lunch* on CNN for about a year. It is still on! There have been some stock market tumbles over the years, and I credit my keen noontime training to missing at least two of those falls.

Whether you choose to invest in savings accounts, CDs, the stock market or cryptocurrency, do your research and decide which fits your finances and your lifestyle the best. Get to know if you want short-term investments or longer-term returns. Many banks offer free financial advice. There are numerous websites to help with finances (see references section). Explore your possibilities. Congratulations on choosing to save your money.

Purchasing Auto Insurance

Most states require that you carry auto insurance. The purpose of car insurance is to cover you if you get into an auto accident that causes injuries to you or another person. It may also cover harm to your personal property or other's property. It also covers theft of the car and items in the car; it depends on the policy you select. You could be responsible for the other driver and occupants if they sustain injuries, or if you damage their car, fence, or other property.

Shop around for an auto insurance policy that suits your needs. Different states have different amounts of insurance you must carry. Check with the motor vehicle department in your state. You can also check online at www.insure.com, then click on the Auto tab.

You want to pick a policy that at least covers the state minimum amount required to carry for insurance. Then you want to decide how much to insure your car for. You can look at Kelley Blue Book online (www.kbb.com) to determine what your car is worth on the market today.

It is very important to figure out what your current assets are when you start to gain them, such as a savings account, stocks, houses, cars, boats, and other belongings. You can lose all the above if you are sued for damages and do not have adequate insurance.

Here are the different elements of what is offered through auto insurance:

- **Collision Coverage.** This pays for damage to your car after an accident.
- Comprehensive Coverage. Covers non-collision damage like theft, vandalism, fire, and many natural disasters to your auto.
- **Liability Coverage.** Covers property damage and injuries that you caused.
- Uninsured/Underinsured Motorists Coverage. Covers you if the other driver is at fault and has no insurance or too little insurance.
- **Personal Injury Protection / Medical Payments.** Covers medical expenses no matter who is at fault.
- **Auto Rental.** Provides a rental vehicle while your car is being repaired.
- **Tow Service.** Provides such services as changing tires, charging batteries, and towing (to home, mechanic, or body shop, usually within a five-mile radius).

Consider new car replacement insurance if you are purchasing a brand-new car. To qualify for this coverage, your new car must fit into these criteria:

- The car must be less than two years old.
- You must be the original owner.
- The car must have less than 15,000 miles on it.

This is an insurance add-on. It allows you to replace your car if totaled (when the damage exceeds the purchase price of the car). It also covers theft of your auto. You may replace it with a new auto that is the same or most like your car that was damaged or stolen.

Another option to consider is guaranteed asset protection (GAP) insurance, an add-on pays for the amount of money you still owe on your car loan. This is paid on the actual cash value of your auto at the time of the theft or damage minus depreciation for time you have used of your car. Insurers consider factors such as mileage, age of the car, condition, and local prices for similar cars.

Spend time learning about the rates for insurance in your area. The range of costs often depends on your age and driving record. Typically, rates are higher for young adults.

You can do the following to potentially lower the cost of auto insurance:

- Get good grades in school, either high school or college.
- Take driver's training or driver's education courses.
- Maintain a good driving record.
- Do not get into accidents or receive moving violation tickets.
- Renew your driver's license on time and register your car. Have it tested (smog test, environmental test, etc.) before your registration is due. Different states require this to be done within a given period, such as within six weeks before registering.
- Do not drink or do drugs while operating a motor vehicle.
- Wear your glasses if needed for driving.
- Don't drink, eat, or smoke.
- Don't text while driving.

If you haven't purchased a car yet, consider purchasing a used vehicle since insurance is not as costly. Keep your driver's license, vehicle registration and proof of insurance accessible whenever you are driving.

Enjoy driving. Don't be distracted by your phone, don't text, and don't fiddle with your music, as all these things can lead you to have an accident. Most cities have anti-racing laws prohibiting people from racing on public streets. Many communities have raceways that are owned privately and allow people to race there. Be safe! Take care of your auto. It's an investment in your ability to have autonomy.

CHAPTER 5

Caring for Your Health: Physical and Mental Well-Being

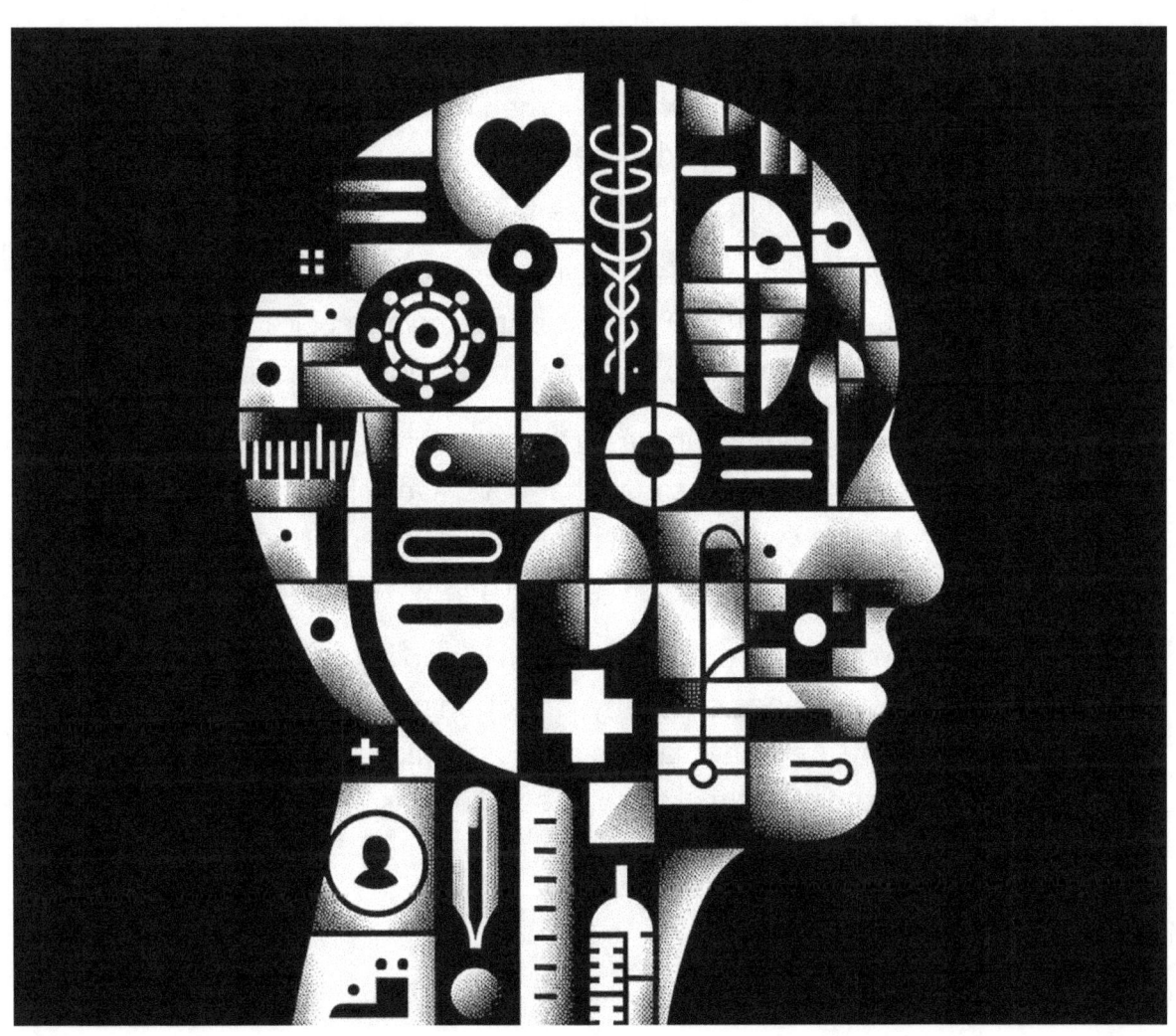

Your health is very important to take care of. Now, being on your own, you will be responsible for taking action when you are not feeling well. This chapter will walk you through where to find care, how to find a professional, when it is urgent to be seen, how to get health insurance, and more.

Medical Insurance

Since you are a human, you likely will need medical assistance sometime in your young life. It may be for a twisted ankle, illness, emergency hospital assistance, annual check-up, or lab work (blood test, urine test, etc.).

Whatever it is, you need to know where to get these services in your area, and when they are open. They usually ask for ID (license or passport), medical insurance card (if insured), and a payment or copay, so be sure to have those accessible when needed.

If you have insurance through your parent's medical plan, you will need to find an alternative when you turn twenty-six, as that coverage will terminate at the year's end. Some states will allow you to be included on your parents' coverage until age thirty. For further information, you can go to https://www.healthcare.gov/.

Have a plan for when you "age out" of your family's policy. You may purchase your own policy from an insurance company, or you might be able to get insurance through your job. There are many plans to choose from, so try to find coverage that is affordable for you and offers extras you need, such as:

- Dental care
- Prescriptions

- Eyecare
- Physical therapy
- Mental health care

Here are the main types of insurance to choose from.

Lowest Monthly Premium

- You pay the least amount of money for your monthly premium.
- You pay the highest amount of money for services.
- You most likely would have to pay thousands of dollars for your deductible. A deductible is a set amount to be paid before insurance begins to cover your costs.

    Example: If you need surgery and a hospital stay that cost $14,000, and your annual deductible is $6,000, you would pay the $6,000 deductible, and your insurance would pay a percentage of the balance of allowed costs.

- This type of plan usually has no other benefits with it and may not pay for anything but illness or injury. Preventive care (regular check-ups, immunizations, mammograms, etc.) generally isn't included.

Moderate Monthly Premiums

- The moderate premium is a bit more costly than the lowest monthly payment listed above.
- The deductibles are usually lower than the above plan. Your out-of-pocket expenses are also less.
- The amount of care you receive is elevated, and they usually pay for routine preventive care. Sometimes this type of plan will pay for a portion of your medications.

High Monthly Premiums

- Plans with high monthly premiums typically start covering you right away. This means that you won't have to wait long periods before your insurance starts paying for medical costs.
- Immediate coverage can be particularly beneficial for those who require frequent medical care or have pre-existing conditions that necessitate ongoing, more frequent treatment.
- There are lower deductibles and copays.
- There may be more perks, such as the ability to make appointments with specialists without getting your doctor's pre-approval.
- May be more cost-effective if you do have chronic issues.

Terminology for Health Care Plans

- **Premium.** This is a monthly enrollment fee you pay, which is dependent on the medical plan you choose.
- **Copayments.** Amount you are responsible for each time you receive medical care.
- **Deductible.** The amount you need to pay before your insurance will pay for covered services. The insurance then shares the total cost with you.
- **Cap (Out-of-Pocket Expenses).** This is the amount of money you must spend before insurance payments will cover 100 percent of your medical costs.
- **HMO (Health Maintenance Organization).** A program where doctors work for the HMO network. You are typically required to see doctors or hospitals within the network, though emergency situations are usually covered at out-of-network facilities.
- **PPO (Preferred Provider Organization).** You have a larger pool of doctors to choose from. You are often allowed to be seen without a referral for a specialist outside the network. You may need to pay a higher copayment for such services.

- **Preventive Care.** This type of care is aimed at preventing illness or discovering illness. It can include the following: wellness visits, mammograms, diabetes education, wellness visits, blood work, screenings for diseases, immunizations, gynecological visits, and more.

> Member ID: 00297431173
> Group Number: D86250119
>
> *Pacific Caring HMO*
>
> Member Name: Shelly Lauren Rosen
>
> Plan: HMO 2, Dental

Front of card

- **Member ID.** Your specific number assigned to you.
- **Group Number.** Identifies your plan or benefit package.
- **Member Name.** This name will be the name you must use for all your health services.
- **Plan Number.** Helps doctors and hospitals know your coverage, deductibles, and billing needs. It also helps assure that your claims are processed correctly.

> **Pacific Caring HMO Customer Service Center**
>
> **Redwood City:** 650-007-0000 Outpatient & Hospital
>
> **Sacramento:** 916-006-9000 Dental
>
> **Ask A Nurse**
> (member's 24 hour service) 1-888-000-2222
>
> **Send claims to:** Claims Service, PO Box 000, Sacramento, CA 94299

Back of Card

The back of your card typically contains contact information, special services (e.g., Ask-A-Nurse) information, and information on where claims should be sent.

Government Run Medical Insurance

Disclaimer: As of May 25, 2025, due to a change in governmental administration, the following programs may not be available. This may change at any given point in the future. Check with the organizations listed below in your area for more information.

If you are a United States citizen living in the US who is not incarcerated, you may be eligible for free or reduced-cost health insurance coverage through Affordable Care Act's Health Insurance Marketplace (www.usa.gov and www.healthcare.gov).

You also may be eligible for state-run Medicaid programs. If you think you may meet the low-income threshold for your state, check with your local Medicaid office and fill out the required forms to see if you qualify (www.healthcare.gov).

University hospitals, centers, and clinics, commuinty health centers, and some Urgent Care clinics may offer a sliding scale (payment based on your income) as well as walk-in health care services.

Hospital emergency rooms are required (in the US) to treat people who have no insurance. While they may care for you, whether you have income or not, you still could be responsible to make payments in the future.

The Department of Health in your area may provide services such as vaccinations, tests, and screenings free of charge.

For lower-cost dental services, look into dentist training programs. Some dental offices also participate in a dental insurance pool, which means prices are often preset and discounted compared to customary dental fees. I found an application in my dentist's office, and it was offered through a credit union. The yearly fee was quite a bit less than going to get individual coverage through a dental insurance company.

The Importance of Seeking Health Care

When we are young, we tend to think of ourselves as invincible. It truly seems that way when we can stay up all night with seemingly no consequences!

But even if it feels that way, listen to your body and make good decisions when taking care of yourself. Your body is with you for life.

If you are experiencing medical or mental health issues, it is important to know when to seek help. It is best to set up regular health exams. Once a year may be sufficient if you have no chronic issues. Otherwise, an exam every few months and lab work may be needed to help diagnose and treat conditions to prevent chronic conditions from worsening.

If you experience symptoms for a couple of weeks, it is wise to seek a medical professional. Catching a condition early could help it from becoming chronic. Continual fatigue, high blood pressure, ongoing pain, losing or gaining weight with no apparent reason, shortness of breath, bladder or bowel issues, an injury to a body part, frequent coughing, or fever above 100.4 degrees Fahrenheit may be a few reasons to make an appointment right away.

Go to the hospital emergency room if you are experiencing any of the following:

- A severe allergic reaction where your throat is swelling, you have a skin reaction, or you are experiencing a severe digestive reaction to something you ingested
- Symptoms that may indicate a heart attack (pain in your left arm, pain in your chest, and shortness of breath)
- Stroke symptoms (paralysis, trouble speaking, inability to raise both arms over one's head, one arm becomes weak and cannot stay up, blurry vision, difficulty walking, or severe, sudden headache)
- Severe fever of 104 degrees Fahrenheit or more
- A potential broken bone
- A seizure, blow to the head, or unconsciousness
- Strong, consistent pain in your body

Mental Health

I worked in the mental health field for eighteen years. It was a rewarding experience to help people of all ages delve into their issues and courageously move forward in life.

For some people, it was a struggle to be vulnerable and express feelings with words that were difficult to find.

For others it was exciting to learn about themselves. They came each week with a thirst to take another step, to find what was previously unknown.

Having self-assurance, being open about yourself, knowing what you want in life, and contributing to relationships are skills that people strive for. In attaining this, you will know yourself. But getting there isn't necessarily an obvious road. Everyone has their own circumstances and experiences. It's what makes us all unique.

Some people grow up equipped with more tools to function in the world. Other people struggle to grasp how to move past difficult childhoods, broken relationships, poverty, a lack of support or direction, and self-doubt.

Many people feel depressed, hopeless, sad, and confused about how to deal with certain issues. Others may feel angry, alone, or anxious. When these feelings begin to overshadow functioning well in life, it is reasonable to want resolution—to feel better.

Maybe you need help boosting your self-esteem or dealing with a crisis. We all have knee-jerk emotional reactions throughout the day, but if you have difficulty balancing these emotions with accomplishing what you need to feel good in life, it may be time for you to find a professional to talk to. No one likes the feeling of being stuck.

Feelings are complex, and it is never "bad" to have them. If you are lost or hurting, find someone you can rely on to help you through those issues. Your emotional welfare is as important as any other aspect of life. Look for a therapist who is a licensed marriage and family counselor, a clinical psychologist, or a psychiatrist (MFC, PhD, or MD). Always do your research and get recommendations if you can.

You can get therapy in person or online, so pick what works for you. There are also community mental health facilities available. You may also talk with a school counselor if you are currently enrolled.

If you are feeling suicidal, notice escalating feelings of sadness, are experiencing frequent episodes of agitation, have difficulty sleeping, notice a loss of interest in things that were recently appealing to you, or have feelings to harm yourself, please contact a clinic or go to a hospital emergency room. The National Suicide Hotline number is 988.

Mental health is important to your well-being. There is no reason to feel embarrassed or ashamed to reach out for mental health services. You deserve to have a place to work out issues. Many people from every culture and every socioeconomic group seek guidance from a professional counselor. Every age group is a part of the client base.

When you visit a mental health practitioner, you will arrange an appointment to see the clinician of your choosing. You may initially speak to someone who does intake. This person gets general information from you and may ask what brings you to seek assistance.

When in your session, your clinician may ask you again about what brought you to the therapy session. You will have the opportunity to converse with one another and to set up a meeting schedule for counseling. There are several styles of therapy, and you will want to find someone you feel comfortable expressing yourself with.

You can ask questions, but know that therapy is a process that evolves as you trust the therapist and feel able to open up. Therapy can help you explore issues that prevent you from blossoming into the person you wish to be. You will have an opportunity to work with your therapist to understand how your inner workings affect your day-to-day interactions.

Finding a Provider for Health Services

Depending on the type of insurance you have, you may be limited to specific hospitals and groups of providers.

Many insurance companies allow you to pick a primary care provider to oversee your care. When you get lab tests or see specialists, your primary care provider receives those reports and consults with the specialists as needed to give you feedback on your care.

Your primary care provider should be someone you feel comfortable discussing important issues with. Ask friends for recommendations if needed. Sites online also rate doctors based on their patients' responses on questionnaires, which can be another valuable source of information. Another option is to ask other health professionals you know for recommendations.

It is important that you find practitioners who listen to you, especially when you have questions. Each visit, I usually have a list of topics to cover:

- Questions
- Tests or vaccinations available
- Referrals needed
- Issues about medications (if I am taking any)
- Current medical concerns

On your first visit with your primary care provider, the doctor or nurse will ask about you and your family's medical history.

Knowing this medical information ahead of time will make things easier. Don't put off gathering it since it may take time to put together. Create a folder that contains the following:

- **Information About Family Members and Illnesses They Have Had.** Be sure to indicate each person's relationship to you: your maternal grandfather and maternal grandmother (mother's parents), paternal grandfather and paternal grandmother (father's parents), mother, father, and siblings. Include illnesses, surgeries, childhood illnesses, allergies, hospital stays, and so on for each person. Do the best you can based on memory, especially when records aren't available.
- **Your Own Medical History.** This should contain your current illnesses, injuries, tests, childhood illnesses, hospitalizations, and vaccines received. If available, have records and doctor contact numbers listed in case your current doctor needs to reference previous information. If you have test results, X-rays, scans, or biopsy reports, add them to your folder. You can also request additional copies of records by contacting the Patient Records Department of the location you received your services.

Your Medical Team

Several professionals make up your medical team:

- Doctors (general Practitioners or specialists)
- Registered Nurses (RN), advanced nurse practitioners (APRN, nurses who are trained to do some of the tasks that a doctor can do, such as prescribe medicine and make diagnoses), and nurses' aides (who assist RNs)
- Technical assistants (who perform uncomplicated tasks under the supervision of doctors and nurses)

When you visit the doctor's office, you will need to bring your insurance card (if insured), your ID, and copay (your designated portion charged for services up front).

Often you will have to fill out various forms and sign them. One form asks for your permission to bill the insurance company (if you have one). You will also fill out a form that designates you (or maybe a parent) as the person responsible for payments; copays not covered by your insurance carrier.

You will also fill out a Health Insurance Portability and Accountability (HIPPA) form. Signing this form gives the doctor, doctor's office, or hospital permission to share your information with people you designate as your representative or with other doctors. The HIPPA Act protects patients from nonassigned persons requesting or viewing your medical records. By signing a HIPPA form, you acknowledge that a person can only view your records with your permission. Ask the receptionist for more information if needed.

Your doctor is there to help you understand any issues you are dealing with. That includes best practices for your care, choices of medications (if needed), treatment plans, follow-ups, how to understand your test results, getting referrals, and more.

It is your job to make sure you understand. If you are unclear about anything, be sure to ask for further explanations. You are best at taking care of yourself when you have clarity to follow through. It is your body, so make sure you speak up if needed! Advocate for yourself. Ask questions.

CHAPTER 6
Living a Healthy Life

Many people wait until middle age to get enthused about health, but there is no time like right now to start developing healthy habits. I started my healthy habits when I was three. I loved to dance any chance I could. Sometimes moments from our childhood can reinforce the healthy habits we should embrace right now.

As a child, I would visit my grandparents on holidays and in the summer. Since I swam from morning until night, I got slathered with suntan lotion to protect my easily burned skin. My grandfather would drop me off at 10:00 a.m. and pick me up at 5:00 p.m. I had an inflatable ring, and I would paddle that thing all over the pool. Sonoma, California was very rural then. My grandfather chose fresh vegetables and fruit at the fruit stand to take home. Not only did I learn the importance of sunscreen, but I learned to love vegetables and fruit. Now I eat a plant-based diet and have all the vegetables I want!

While you may see yourself as young, consider that the body you have is the body that you will live in for the rest of your life. Older people today frequently live to their late seventies or eighties, and thanks to advances in medical science, the youth of today may live well into their nineties and hundreds. All the more reason to care for your body now.

There is so much we now know about how the body works that was unknown fifty years ago. Here are some examples. A CAT (CT) scan, which stands for *computed tomography*, takes a three-dimensional picture of the inside of your body. It can take very precise images to help identify issues and make diagnoses.

MRIs (magnetic resonance imaging) have helped us get more accurate views into the body by using very strong magnets and radio waves to produce detailed images.

Now we have microbiome analysis (this closely examines the bacteria in targeted parts of your body like the gut and mouth) to see how they are working in your body, and if needed, what can help you to improve your health.

DNA (deoxyribonucleic acid) is the code that identifies your individual makeup. Your genome is the specific aspects of the code that make up your DNA. It is a molecule which tells your body how to operate and is found in nearly all your cells.

Unless you were born as an identical twin or another multiple birth, no one else will have the same code as you. Your genome remains the same your entire life, acting as instructions, guiding your body to work. Science is moving swiftly to identify genomic issues, understand diseases, and find cures through DNA research.

Developing vaccines to fight viruses that have yet to receive a vaccine and evolving vaccines currently in use has become an area in which there is great hope for breakthroughs.

Stem cell therapy enables stem cells to become multiple types of cells within your body. They are somewhat of a blank slate. A stem cell can turn into cells that can help repair such things as damaged nerves or tissue after a brain injury. Stem cells can be harvested from bone marrow to help address blood diseases.

Stem cells can also be collected from a baby's umbilical cord after birth. They can be saved and used if the child has certain issues. Stem cells are used to repair parts of the body. They have been used to reverse heart disease; they are used in bone marrow transplants (known as hematopoietic stem cells) and to reconstruct the immune system. Medical researchers have discovered numerous other diseases and issues to target.

Artificial intelligence (AI) is used to devise treatment plans, analyze scans (such as X-rays), provide virtual assistance to patients, and help with the intricacies of robotic surgery. AI can analyze large amounts of data to help assess new drugs. This is just the tip of the iceberg in naming a few areas AI can help with.

3D printing uses a special printer to recreate objects out of plastic or other materials. It is often used in the medical field to produce implants and prosthetics that can be configured to fit exactly to an individual patient's body. This process can fabricate intricate medical devices.

The world has new discoveries and innovations year by year. You will potentially live longer than most of the generations before you. Let's examine some of the areas that can allow you to live your healthiest life as we move into the next sections.

The Importance of Sleep

So many people push themselves to operate on less sleep than is recommended. Maybe they feel pressure from the demands of life (work, studying, and social and family requirements). Maybe it's to enjoy the night life. But whether you are a night owl or an early bird, you need to assess what is a good amount of sleep for you.

The Centers for Disease Control recommends that adults eighteen to sixty years old get seven or more hours of sleep per day. The quality of that sleep is important. People who get sufficient sleep find that they have fewer instances of illness. It can lower your risk of diseases such as high blood pressure and diabetes, and it can improve your mental health and reduce stress. Adequate sleep also can improve concentration and memory.

During sleep, your body and brain get refreshed and repaired. Sleep is also important because you dream during that period. It is believed that one has a rapid eye movement (REM) dream cycle throughout your period of sleep. During REM, your eyes remain active along with muscles surrounding your eyes, while your body does not move. Some suggest this state occurs at least every ninety minutes. While you are asleep, your brain works to organize the information you took in during waking hours, your emotional state, and your reactions to your day. In fact, your brain may be working through issues and examining memories when you dream.

Some people experience sleep disorders that compromise the quality and duration of their sleep. They can interrupt your ability to have restful sleep, cause you to sleep at inappropriate times, or cause you to not sleep at all. These symptoms can be serious and affect your ability to concentrate, operate machinery, and remember things. Severe sleep disorders can even be a threat to your health and quality of life. Some of the disorders related to sleep include the following:

- **Narcolepsy.** Sudden falling asleep and extreme tiredness during waking hours.
- **Restless Leg Syndrome.** Your legs feel uncomfortable or painful while you are sleeping, and you feel that you must move them around.
- **Sleep Apnea.** Shallow breathing, not breathing for several seconds, snoring, or gasping.
- **Insomnia.** Difficulty falling or staying asleep.
- **Sleepwalking.** Walking or performing tasks while remaining asleep, but your eyes are usually open and not taking in the surroundings.

You should visit a sleep specialist or sleep clinic if you have any of these symptoms:

- You are excessively tired during the day, even after having a full night's sleep.
- You wake up several times at night.
- You frequently feel unrested when waking up from at least a six-hour sleep.
- You have difficulty breathing at night, you snore, or you stop breathing or gasp for air.
- You have difficulty falling asleep or staying asleep.
- You have frequent periods of increased movement during sleep.

Many doctors prioritize sleep as the first and most important step to becoming healthy. Here are some tips that may help you to maintain optimal sleep:

- Try to sleep around the same time daily.
- Sleep in darkened, quiet rooms conducive to having a restful sleep.
- Sleep in cooler rooms, which may be more helpful for comfortable sleep than rooms kept at warmer temperatures.

- Keep a tidy area around your bed. This signals to your brain that the bed is a restful place.
- Eat and watch TV in separate areas.
- After noon, opt for noncaffeinated beverages: water, sugar-free sodas, carbonated water, or herbal tea.
- Before bedtime, limit eating to light snacks (such as a piece of fruit, a small salad, a piece of toast, or a small bowl of cereal). Stay away from eating a heavy meal before sleeping. Pick something that is not salty, sugary, or loaded with fats.
- Finish exercising at least three hours before bedtime.
- Avoid smoking and drinking alcohol, as this can affect the quality of your sleep or make it hard for you to fall asleep.
- Avoid napping during the day, which can make it difficult to have a restful sleep at night.
- Know how much sleep your body needs and set your sleep schedule to accommodate that.

Healthy Eating for Your Future

When I was a kid, meals were created with convenience in mind. Canned goods, frozen foods, sugary cereals, breads full of refined flour, lots of red meat (especially ground beef), and drinks loaded with sugar were daily staples. Food had additives and preservatives that later were deemed harmful. It was a time when many people were clueless about what constitutes a healthy diet.

To give you a sense of different types of diets and what they include, I will share my food adventure with you.

In my teens I discovered the vegetarian way of eating (vegetables, grains, fruit, legumes, and dairy products).

Then I switched to a macrobiotic diet in my college years. This diet, based in Eastern philosophy, focused on eating foods predominantly grown in the area where you live, mostly plant based with grain, vegetables, fruit, nuts, beans, legumes, fermented foods, and some fish. Then my doctor told me I was getting too thin and likely malnourished. That ended that. I don't think I understood how to combine the food to get proper nutrients.

For many years I liked the Mediterranean diet. The name comes from the menus taken from countries bordering the Mediterranean Sea (vegetables, grains, legumes, olive oil, fish, seafood, dairy, poultry, eggs, and meat).

My favorite countries were Spain, Portugal, and Morocco. I went there every year over a seven-year period. I learned to use lemon and olive oil (the dressings for all the salads I had) instead of butter and heavy sauces.

I made several types of paella (a Spanish dish) with seafood, chicken, vegetables, and saffron with rice, and I varied the ingredients. Chicken and fish were always cooked in olive oil—lots of it! In both Spain and Portugal, the fish (shrimp too) was always fresh caught and served with polenta, rice, or couscous. Chicken was often part of a stew with potatoes served with vegetables.

Moroccan dishes tended to have more spices, vegetables, meat, yams, chicken, lamb, and grains. Sometimes the items were served with dried apricots, currants, and nuts served on rice or couscous. The wonderful seasonings were easily found at the local outdoor markets.

I was a vegetarian (vegetables, fruits, legumes, grains, and dairy products).

At one point I added fish and seafood to the above, and this is called a pescatarian diet.

Now I have settled on eating a plant-based diet. With a focus on unprocessed foods, this diet is one of the healthiest diets one can eat. It is rich in nutrients and low in empty calories. It provides healthy levels of vitamins, minerals, and antioxidants. Additionally it adds fiber to your diet. Plant-based diets have been found to lower risk of heart disease, type 2 diabetes, some cancers (breast cancer, colorectal, and prostate cancer). It can help with maintaining a healthy body weight. It can help to reduce inflammation in your body. Keep in mind that the plant-based foods that are healthy for you are not made of white flour, added sugar, or heavily processed ingredients. Vegan junk food that is fried or imitation meat often has a bunch of additives. Always check nutrition food labels and eat minimally processed foods to get the highest positive outcome.

It helps one avoid eating livestock that has received antibiotics and other medication while they are being kept in unsanitary, cramped environments. This includes fish, which have also had their run in with unhealthy additives through fish farming on land in large tanks or ponds and in open-sea netted enclosures, where fish are given antibiotics and exposed to disinfectants added to the water. (This practice has been known to pollute the waters and affect the sea life in neighboring areas.)

Plant-based diets are also good for the environment. It saves animals since they are not slaughtered as part of the diet. Likewise, since soybeans, corn, and less-nutritious grains are not grown to feed and fatten up animals, it provides more agricultural space for more nutritious foods.

Well, it's been quite the journey. I have always been interested in culinary pursuits. I have followed my different phases in diet with creating tasty meals

Eating a diet that provides the vitamins, nutrients, and minerals your body needs daily can help your body to function at its optimum capacity. The above-mentioned diets are just a few examples of the many choices available. I am not recommending any specific diet; you should find one that fits your personal requirements. Talk to your doctor or nutritionist to help you make an informed decision.

Later, I will share a variety of recipes with you, which I feel fit in with healthy eating. They are also tasty. Healthy eating can be a way to pamper yourself and a way to be social when sharing with others. Treat your body well, and enjoy the deliciousness of healthy eating!

Science, Our Bodies, and the Food We Eat

Food affects our bodies and our health, both with positive effects and harmful effects.

There are many studies suggesting that diets that include vegetables, grains, fruit, and healthy fats in moderation can improve quality of life.

The Mayo Clinic emphasizes that young adults should strive to eat a balanced diet. They suggest that you fill an average-size plate with the following proportions: 1/4 grains, 1/4 lean protein, and 1/2 fruits and vegetables.

Whole grains (brown rice, quinoa, hulled barley, millet, whole wheat, rye, popcorn if air popped, wild rice, and spelt) are rich in nutrients.

Vegetables and fruit add minerals, fiber, and vitamins to your diet. Don't forget leafy greens (spinach, kale, bok choy, chard, and some lettuces) and root vegetables (potatoes, yams, carrots, beets, turnips, rutabagas, and parsnips).

Eat lean proteins (fish, beans, nuts, and chicken). Protein allows you to feel fuller after eating for a longer period. It is also needed to build and repair your muscles.

Choose fats that are healthy for you. These fats will aid in brain and cardiovascular health (avocados, dark chocolate, olive oil, hemp seeds, chia seeds, flax seeds, salmon, flaxseed oil, sardines, edamame/soybeans, and nuts).

Limit your salt intake. It will help you to maintain good heart health, keep blood pressure at the desired rate, maintain a healthy flow of fluids in your body, and help you have healthy kidneys. Having a lower salt intake also helps protect your bone growth and bone density. Watch out for salty, processed foods like chips, canned foods, fast foods, and food you get when dining out. Salt is used as a flavor enhancer in many foods. Choosing a low-salt diet can help maintain your health.

Curb your appetite for sugar. Sugar is in many processed food items. It is important to limit your sugar intake for a number of reasons. Too much sugar can lead to unhealthy weight gain; sugar-added sodas are a big culprit. Over a period of time, ingesting too much sugar can lead to insulin resistance and diabetes. Sugar can increase problems with blood pressure and cholesterol levels. It can also cause mood swings when the energy boost wears off, leading to drowsiness. Ultimately, having a sweet tooth may lead you to poor diet choices, driving you to pick sugary snacks instead of healthy foods.

Last, but extremely important for your body to function well, is to drink fluids. It is recommended that you drink eight cups (64 ounces) of fluid every day. Healthy drinks include water, milk, sugarless or low-sugar juice, herbal tea, and electrolyte drinks.

Without proper hydration, you may find your energy level depleting easily. Being hydrated helps you be attentive and able to concentrate. Fluids also help with digestion and taking nutrients into your system. This protects your skin from being dry and ensures proper kidney function.

Next, we will look at reading food ingredient and nutrition labels. This will aid you in deciding what is the best choice for your daily diet. Here's a big tip: Limit your intake of sugar, unhealthy fats, and salt!

I will give you information regarding what nutrients our bodies need daily and how to choose foods to stay healthy.

How to Read a Food Label

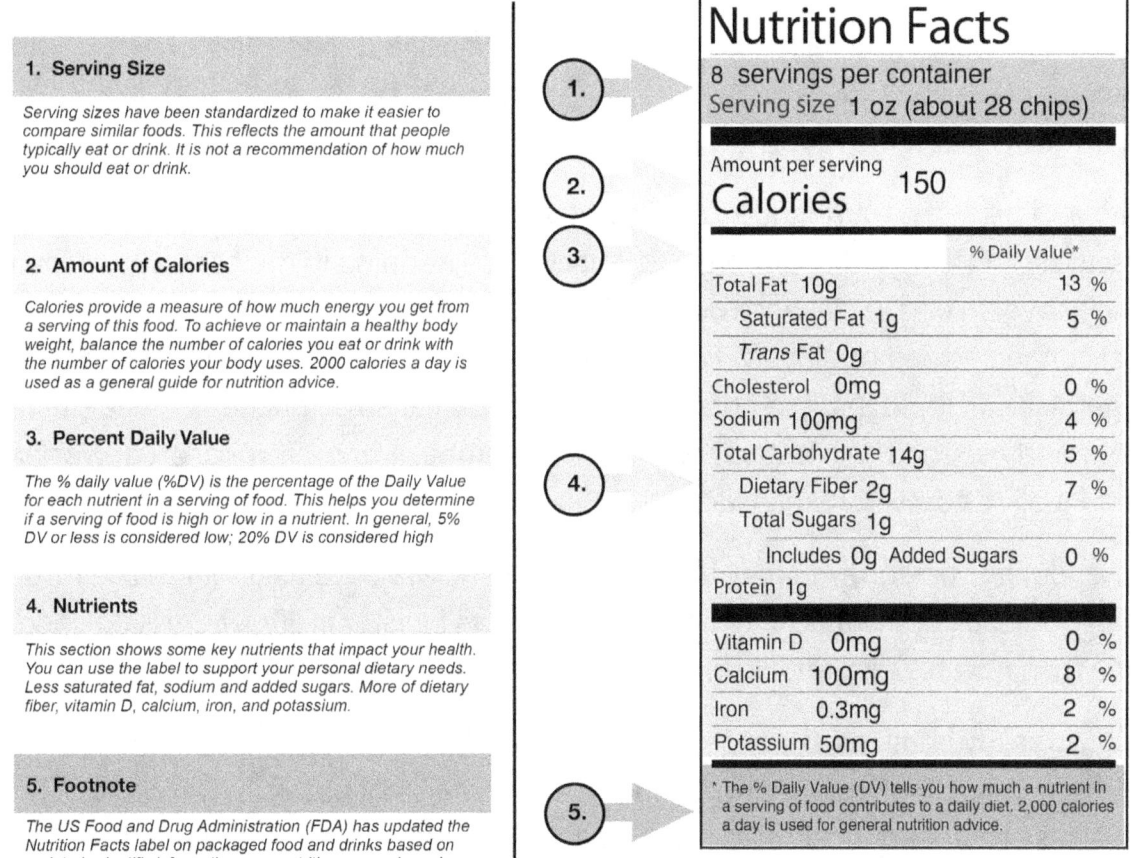

Blue Zones

Dan Buettner is a demographer, someone who studies populations of people to understand how they change over time, what their habits are, and how their characteristics as a group affect birth rates, death rates, and other changes within their community.

Dan wanted to find the source of longevity in certain groups, so he worked with National Geographic and a team of well-known doctors and other experts on a quest to identify the habits of five groups of people living in areas where people lived longer, healthier lives than most. These areas, called Blue Zones, included:

- Loma Linda, California
- Sardinia, Italy
- Ikaria, Greece
- Okinawa, Japan
- Nicoya Peninsula, Costa Rica

Dan and his team found Blue Zone communities have lower instances of chronic diseases, and they walk frequently as opposed to hopping in the car to do errands. They have strong social networks within their community, which allows them to feel connected and not lonely. They eat a mainly plant-based diet with lots of grains, vegetables, fruit, beans, and nuts. Some groups do eat small portions of meat. They frequently spend their last years as active members of their local area, working continually as they become elders.

As a younger person, you may think that you can always be healthier in the future. But good habits can influence how healthy you can be later in life. There is no sooner time than now to start. People living in Blue Zones model habits you can adopt today:

- Eat mostly plant-based, nonprocessed foods rich with grains, beans, and vegetables.
- Move as part of your daily routine. Walk as much as possible. Garden or clean house to get physical activity each day. Participate in local activities like dance, swimming, hiking, dog walking, and so on.
- Be social in your community. Build connections and strong friendships. Spend time with family. Stay connected.
- Find your passion. Have a reason to feel excited every day. Do what you are meant to do.
- Learn to relax. Do not allow yourself to carry stress. Learn to write in your journal, meditate, socialize, move your body, and do breathing exercises. Continued stress can be harmful to your health.
- Eat in moderation. Eat more slowly and let yourself enjoy the food you are eating without overeating. Aim to be 80 percent full.

The above describes how you can live your life fully—and healthily. Start with the areas that are most likely to improve your life now. Then continue to add the other areas so you can live more successfully as you age. You are the holder of your well-being.

The Life Guide You Actually Need

Recipes

Three Bean Chile

Serves 8–10

Lots of ingredients but worth the time. A delicious, simple meal using one large pot.

(*In New Mexico, they spell red and green chiles with an e at the end.*)

Ingredients

- 1 tablespoon olive oil (or water)
- 1 yellow onion
- 4 cloves minced garlic
- 1 sweet potato, cubed
- 6 carrots, sliced
- 2 red bell peppers, chopped
- 1 teaspoon cumin
- ½ teaspoon cinnamon
- 1 teaspoon salt
- 1 teaspoon pepper
- 2 tablespoons unsweetened cacao powder
- 2 tablespoons hot chile powder
- 1 tablespoon paprika
- 1 28 ounce can diced tomatoes
- 1 cup fresh cherry tomatoes, halved
- ¼ cup tomato paste
- 1 cup vegetable broth or water
- 1 4 ounce can chipotle peppers in adobo sauce, chopped
- 1 tablespoon balsamic vinegar
- 1 tablespoon soy sauce or liquid aminos
- 1 14 ounce can pinto beans, drained
- 1 14 ounce can black beans, drained
- 1 14 ounce can kidney beans, drained
- 1 cup yellow sweet corn
- 2 cups baby spinach, roughly chopped
- ½ bunch cilantro, chopped
- 1 lime, juiced
- 1 tablespoon maple syrup

Optional Additions

One pound of ground beef or chicken. Serve with shredded cheddar cheese sprinkled on top. Add sliced avocados

Note

Be sure to adjust the "heat" of your chile as you go. Add a smaller amount of chile powder, cumin, paprika, pepper, and chipotle peppers to start. Let it cook a bit, taste, and adjust to your liking.

Directions

1. Heat olive oil or water in a large pot.
2. Add onion and garlic and sauté until fragrant.
3. Add sweet potatoes, carrots, and bell peppers; sauté 7 minutes.
4. Add all seasonings. Add more oil or water if needed.
5. Pour in tomatoes, broth (or water), tomato paste, chipotle peppers, balsamic vinegar, and soy sauce.
6. Stir to combine.
7. Add all beans.
8. Bring to a boil, then reduce heat and simmer for 15 minutes.
9. Add all remaining ingredients and stir to combine.
10. Gently simmer until the corn is heated through, the tomatoes have softened, and the spinach has wilted.
11. Season to taste by adjusting sriracha, maple syrup, salt, pepper, and lime juice.
12. Enjoy!

Baked Rice Confetti

Serves 4–6

A colorful dish to accompany any meal.

Ingredients

- 4 teaspoons extra-virgin olive oil
- 2 onions, finely chopped
- 1 teaspoon table salt
- 2 ¼ cups water
- 1 cup vegetable broth
- 1 ½ cups long-grain brown rice
- 1 cup pecans, coarsely chopped
- 1 ½ tablespoons chives, dried or fresh
- 1 cup spinach leaves, stemmed and finely chopped
- ¾ cup jarred red peppers, rinsed, patted dry, and chopped

Directions

1. Heat oven to 375 degrees Fahrenheit.
2. In a large pot, sauté onions, and salt with oil until soft and browned.
3. Add water and broth. Bring to a boil.
4. Add rice, pecans, chives, and spinach.
5. Transfer rice mixture to a large, covered baking dish.
6. Bake about 60 minutes until rice is tender and the liquid is absorbed.
7. Remove from oven.
8. Sprinkle peppers over rice, cover, and let sit 5 minutes.
9. Fluff gently to combine. Season with salt and pepper to taste.

Banana Bread

Serves 8–10 (one loaf)

One of the best tasting banana breads I've ever tasted.

Ingredients

- 2 cups all-purpose flour
- ¾ cup sugar
- ¾ teaspoon baking soda
- ½ teaspoon table salt
- ½ cup pecans coarsely chopped
- 3 ripe but firm bananas, peeled
- 6 tablespoons vegetable oil (avocado, sunflower)
- ⅓ cup plain plant-based or dairy yogurt
- 1 tablespoon lemon juice
- 2 teaspoons vanilla extract

Directions

1. Heat oven to 350 degrees Fahrenheit.
2. Grease loaf pan.
3. Whisk together flour, sugar, baking soda, and salt in a large bowl.
4. Stir in nuts. Set aside.
5. In a separate bowl, mash bananas with a fork until slightly lumpy.
6. Stir in oil, yogurt, lemon juice, and vanilla.
7. Gently fold banana mixture into flour mixture until just combined.
8. Transfer batter to loaf pan and smooth top.
9. Bake about 1 hour, or until the top is firm and deep golden.
10. Transfer to a wire rack until completely cool, about 3 hours, before serving.

Options

Add ½ cup of any (or all) of the following ingredients for extra pizzazz: raisins, chocolate chips, or unsweetened shredded coconut.

Thai Chicken Noodle Soup

Serves 4

A very tasty one-dish meal.

Ingredients

- 1 tablespoon vegetable oil
- 2 cloves garlic, minced
- 1 tablespoon fresh ginger, grated
- 2 tablespoons red curry paste (adjust to taste)
- 2 tablespoons peanut butter
- 4 cups chicken broth
- 1 tablespoon Thai basil
- 1 13.5-ounce coconut milk
- 1 tablespoon fish or soy sauce
- 1 teaspoon brown sugar
- 2 boneless, skinless chicken breasts, thinly sliced
- 1 cup mushrooms
- 1 cup baby spinach or bok choy
- 1 cup snow peas, green beans, or long beans
- 5 ounces rice noodles
- juice of 1 lime
- 1 tablespoon chili flakes (optional: adjust to taste)
- Garnish: fresh cilantro, green onions, or chives

Directions

1. In a large pot, sauté the garlic and ginger in oil for 1–2 minutes.
2. Stir in the curry paste and peanut butter; sauté another minute or so.
3. Pour in the chicken broth and Thai basil and bring to a simmer.
4. Add coconut milk, fish sauce, and sugar.
5. Add sliced chicken and simmer 8–10 minutes until cooked through.
6. Add all vegetables and cook until tender, 2–3 minutes.
7. While soup simmers, in a separate pot, cook the rice noodles according to package instructions and set aside.
8. Adjust flavor of soup to taste by adding lime juice, fish sauce, salt, or seasonings.
9. Divide cooked noodles into bowls. Ladle soup over noodles, and top with cilantro, green onions, and chili flakes if desired.

Options

For a different protein, substitute bacon seitan, shrimp, or tofu for the chicken.

Tabouleh

Serves 6–8

An easy-to-make Mediterranean salad to accompany meat dishes and vegetable dishes or to enjoy solo.

Ingredients

- ¾ cup couscous, dry
- 1 ½ cups water
- 2 cups parsley, chopped
- ½ cup scallions, finely chopped
- ¼ cup mint, finely chopped
- ¼ cup olive oil
- 2 tablespoons lemon juice
- 1 ½ teaspoons salt
- ½ teaspoon ground black pepper
- 2 firm, ripe tomatoes, diced (small pieces)
- ¼ cup lemon juice mixed with ½ teaspoon salt

Directions

1. Bring water to a boil. Add couscous and cover, then remove from heat.
2. Wash parsley, remove thick stalks, and chop coarsely.
3. When cool, put couscous in a mixing bowl.
4. Add scallions, parsley, and mint.
5. Beat olive oil with lemon juice and stir in salt and pepper.
6. Add to salad and mix well.
7. Gently stir in tomatoes.
8. Cover and chill for an hour or so before serving.
9. Mix lemon juice and salt in a small bowl and serve. Let individuals add this according to their taste.

Crispy Baked Chicken

Serves 5–6

A family favorite, great for picnics or parties.

Ingredients

- 2 eggs, lightly beaten
- ¼ cup milk
- 1 cup unseasoned fine dry breadcrumbs
- ¾ cup freshly grated Parmesan cheese
- 1 ½ tablespoons dried oregano
- 1 ½ tablespoons dried minced garlic
- 1 ½ tablespoons dried minced onion
- Salt and pepper to taste
- 10 chicken breast halves, thighs, or legs, or combination

Directions

1. Preheat oven to 350 degrees Fahrenheit.
2. In a shallow bowl, stir the eggs and milk together.
3. In a separate bowl, combine the breadcrumbs, cheese, and spices.
4. Dip the chicken pieces in the egg mixture, then into the crumb mixture to coat the chicken sufficiently.
5. Place on a greased baking sheet and bake until meat is tender and the coating is crisp, about 40 minutes.

Chopped Salad

Serves 6

A delicious, fresh salad, like a meal. Serve with your favorite loaf of bread.

Ingredients

- 2 or 3 heads of romaine lettuce, washed and dried
- ⅛ cup olive oil
- ⅛ cup vinegar
- salt and freshly ground pepper to taste
- 6 eggs, hard-boiled, chopped or shredded
- 1 cup chicken, cooked and diced
- 1 cup feta cheese, crumbled
- 1 cup tomatoes, diced
- ½ cup olives, coarsely chopped
- ½ cup walnuts, coarsely chopped
- 1 or 2 avocados, peeled, pitted and sliced

Directions

1. Cut or tear lettuce into bite-sized pieces.
2. Toss lettuce with oil, vinegar, salt, and pepper.
3. Place lettuce in a large salad bowl.
4. Arrange eggs, chicken, cheese, tomatoes, and olives in separate rows on top of lettuce.
5. Evenly sprinkle with walnuts.
6. Arrange avocados on the top of the salad.

Chocolate Avocado Mousse

Ingredients

- 1 cup water
- ¾ cup sugar
- ¼ cup unsweetened cocoa powder
- 1 tablespoon vanilla extract
- ¼ teaspoon tablespoon table salt
- 2 large ripe avocados, halved and pitted
- 3 ½ ounces bittersweet chocolate, chopped

Serves 6

This is a perfectly smooth mousse. It might sound unusual, but the flavor is luscious.

Directions

1. Combine water, sugar, cocoa, vanilla, and salt in a small saucepan.
2. Bring to simmer over medium heat and cook, stirring occasionally, until sugar and cocoa dissolve, about 2 minutes.
3. Remove saucepan from heat and cover to keep warm.
4. Scoop flesh of avocados into a bowl and mash until creamy with a fork.
5. Add warm chocolate mixture and stir until smooth.
6. Microwave the bittersweet chocolate in a bowl, until melted, in 30 second increments.
7. Add melted chocolate to avocado mixture and stir until well mixed.
8. Transfer mousse to a bowl, cover, and refrigerate until chilled and set, at least two hours.

Exercise for Your Health

Exercise is a crucial part of your healthy-living plan. Did you know that just thirty minutes of exercise a day can rejuvenate your body and give you so many overall health benefits? It also helps you to set up a routine that can be put into place throughout your life. Exercise is one of the key factors to keeping your body functioning well and optimally throughout your life.

How you exercise is up to you—just get that body moving! I have loved to dance since I was three years old and followed that passion, taking dance classes in high school and Anna Halprin's Dancer's Workshop in San Francisco. Eventually, I became a dance teacher, co-teaching at the College of Marin in Kentfield, California, as a student assistant, and giving private lessons for disco and ballroom dance. I continue to dance to this day, doing dance aerobics to my favorite high energy music (Sofi Tukker). Dance was always my best way to release emotions and get to my happy place.

Perhaps your preferred exercise involves group sports like pickleball, baseball, or basketball. Or maybe you could take a fancy to doing yoga, dance, or martial arts. You may enjoy the solitude of walking, running, rollerblading or swimming.

Many people have a very active life gardening, painting houses, collecting, and chopping wood.

Any of these activities can help the systems of your body perform better:

- **Endocrine System.** Activity aids in equalizing hormones, such as insulin, endorphins, and cortisol. Exercise increases your metabolic rate by producing hormones that act as regulators. This process helps to maintain or control your weight and can also increase your energy levels.
- **Immune System.** Through exercise, you can increase the flow of immune cells moving through your body, scrubbing clean areas that have bacteria or viruses in them. Immune cells also lower inflammation in your body.

- **Digestive System.** Daily movement helps to stimulate your intestines, which helps prevent constipation. It also helps with regulating hunger and managing your weight. New studies even suggest exercise can help reduce the risk of colon cancer.
- **Nervous System.** Exercise improves brain function by increasing the flow of blood to your brain. This stimulates brain cell growth, boosts cognitive performance, enhances attentiveness, improves memory, and aids decision-making. It also increases the levels of serotonin and dopamine that enhance a state of well-being.
- **Respiratory System.** Aerobic movement requires the lungs to become better at expanding and contracting to inhale oxygen and exhale carbon dioxide. The more you exercise, the more oxygen your body can absorb, strengthening your ability to endure more activity.
- **Lymphatic System.** Exercise helps the lymphatic system move toxins and waste products from the body. This system moves unwanted material from your body through certain lymph nodes, organs, and lymph vessels, supporting immune function and speeding up the detoxification process.
- **Musculoskeletal System.** Weighted exercises help with muscle growth and bone density. Movement helps to keep your joints mobile and flexible.

The above lists let you look at how important exercise is to your body. It is easy to see how helpful exercise is to keep all the systems working!

Choose an exercise program that will keep your interest. You may wish to participate in several forms of exercise and movement. There are so many options.

The important thing is to take care of yourself. Give yourself this key to health by making exercise a lifelong part of your daily routine.

If you have health issues, be sure to meet with your doctor to discuss what type of exercise program would be safe and most beneficial for you.

In this chapter, we've talked about the importance of healthy eating, community, and exercise in living a balanced life. Go through the following list to evaluate your current wellness level:

- Do you eat balanced, healthy meals?
- Do you know what nutrients your body needs?
- How often do you get regular exercise?
- Do you socialize with others?
- What unhealthy habits do you have?
- Do you feel that you spend too much time watching TV, gaming, or using social media?
- What are your sleep habits?
- Are you keeping hydrated?
- Do you pursue things that make you feel fulfilled?

CHAPTER 7
Relationships With Family

There are always questions that come up about family when seeking independence and living on your own. One of my friend's daughters, Rene, age twenty, was concerned that she got phone calls from her mother daily. Some of these calls came at inopportune times when she had friends over or was on her way to a study group. She felt obligated to take the calls, but it was interfering with her sense of control over her own time.

I brought up the idea of setting boundaries with her mother.

She voiced that she thought her mom would get angry or feel rejected. I suggested that she let her mom know that she wants to enjoy their calls together and that it would be better if they could set aside a time or two to talk every week. This way, Rene could get her time with Mom and not feel torn between doing what she had planned or feeling the need to stick around and talk.

Setting boundaries is important in any relationship, especially with family. Sometimes making a situation work depends on your clear communication with one another.

As my grandmother got older, she wanted me to visit frequently. I tried to drive the two-hour-plus round trip at least once every two weeks. Then my job became more demanding, and I could not visit as often. I no longer had time during the week to take an afternoon off. Nonetheless, she felt ignored and unimportant.

I explained my work situation in detail. She mentioned that she did not realize that I worked so many hours. This reassured her that it was not about being unwilling to see her.

Knowing that she would not be around forever, I wanted to figure out a way to connect more often. So I set up phone time with her. She was hard of hearing; I purchased her a special phone that was louder than most. She was pleased. We talked more often, and I rarely heard her complain about my not visiting enough.

By communicating clearly to her, my grandmother learned about my situation, and she was able to adjust her expectations.

As you build your life away from your family, it can be perplexing how to juggle time with friends, time to yourself, and time to visit with family. To maintain these important aspects of your life, you have to find the right balance for you.

Family can be supportive of you and help you to feel grounded by providing a home base to return to, a place of belonging. Friends can help you to explore your new world and discuss experiences you share with them now.

I remember I would often have more than one invitation to go out to do something on a weekend night, especially in my twenties. One friend might be setting up a dinner of mutual friends, and another person would ask me to go on a double date that included my crush. I came to realize I had other days free to get together, so I started to go with the first invite I got. That eliminated my feeling torn between options or feeling like I'd miss out. I learned to feel good with that decision. To this day I follow that rule: First come, first served.

Holidays were always challenging, especially big ones like Christmas. That was my favorite holiday. As a young adult, I always spent the morning and afternoon with my parents. When I had a boyfriend, we would spend Christmas Eve with his family, Christmas Day with mine.

As time went on, I moved back to the same city as my parents. I began to have Christmas celebrations at my house. I invited family members and several friends to join me. I would go with my friends out in the evening. Usually I'd do my favorite thing, dance.

Figuring out how to make new traditions, compromising on how you are spending time, and planning your special time with family will help define your new life. This is a part of the experience of moving forward.

Sometimes conflicts arise within a family. It is often difficult to find comfort when sparring about family matters. If defenses go up, you may not have the type of communication needed to find understanding and resolution.

Sometimes you'll already have an idea about what has caused the conflict. Most of the time, when things get heated, it is due to at least one of you feeling you are not seen or heard.

Active listening is a technique that comes in handy during these moments.

To use it, agree to take turns talking about what you are feeling and what is upsetting to you. Each of you should be an active listener when the other is speaking. You should not interrupt, and you should listen attentively to what the other is saying.

Putting your phone on silent and finding a place to talk privately is helpful. The key to having this method work is to hear each other and to get an understanding of where the other person is coming from, without blame or criticism.

If you want more clarity about something, then you can ask them to tell you more about it, when it is your turn. This is an opportunity to understand one another and share on a level where you can express emotions, feel safe to say what you feel, and potentially move your relationship to a new level.

Every family member is an individual. Their views may be very different from others'. This can happen because of life experience or age differences, but everyone still wants to be respected and valued. Many families have diverse ideas about politics, religion, values, or even seemingly benign issues like what to eat. Try to understand such differences. This does not mean you have to change. But learning about each other is an invaluable opportunity to build unity.

Sometimes family can be the best support system you have. If you feel you have that type of relationship, do not hesitate to reach out to family to help with difficult issues, such as the loss of a relationship, illness, or financial difficulties.

Some people do not have that type of relationship. If this is you, reach out to a friend, educator, counselor, therapist, or other person you feel safe to discuss personal issues with. This support can help you work through these difficulties. If you have deeper issues with family history, seek out a professional to help you work through it.

CHAPTER 8

Seeing the World

73

Why do so many people like to travel? I enjoyed traveling in my teens, twenties, and thirties. Not only did I enjoy adventuring to other countries, but I also visited many cities in different states here in the United States.

I loved seeing different types of geography. The trees, the streams, the fields of wildflowers, and the rivers—they were amazing to me, and so different from what I knew growing up near the ocean.

Starting in my teens I would go backpacking in the mountains with a friend or a group. My favorite experience was smelling the aroma of the campfire and feeling the comradery we had sitting around it eating, talking, singing, and laughing.

My favorite trips were driving up the coast of California, Oregon, Washington, and Southern Canada. On the next trip, we explored the mountains in Nevada, saw the incredible rock formations in Mt. Zion, Utah, stood looking into the Grand Canyon, and experienced the changes in Arizona from mountain coolness to hot deserts.

Taking trips, whether near or far, can help you to feel independent. Planning, exploring, and making decisions as you go are all part of seeing how you adapt to a new environment. This aspect of travel can even help you in your personal growth.

Many of the spots we visited were very different from the more urban life I had experienced. Along the way, we met people of all ages, including Nina, an artist in Arizona. I was so taken by the intricate designs of the rugs she had woven. She sat at a table outside the café with her cup of coffee. She saw that I was interested and asked my friend and me to sit with her.

She told us the story of how she learned to weave in her teenage years. This interaction inspired me to take a textile course and learn to weave myself. That time with Nina was one of the highlights of that trip—a chance meeting with a lovely, creative stranger that changed my life.

Traveling allows for the opportunity to meet new people whose way of life or culture may be different from yours. You can experience their cuisine, customs, art, and architecture, getting an understanding of how they differ and are similar to you. All of this can have a huge impact on your life.

Even experiencing another type of climate is interesting. When we visited Philadelphia, a family member dropped us off at a raised train stop. It was a platform, with no protection from the weather conditions. Snow was coming down, and it was cold—eighteen degrees. A bit hard for a California girl to handle. This was the longest thirty minutes I had ever spent outside braving the elements. I was thankful that I brought a very warm coat.

I was very excited to spend time in New York City, our first destination. When we got to Grand Central Station, we took off to explore the city by foot. A full day was spent, and we marveled at how well we got around in this totally unfamiliar city. I was quite thankful that all the people we met were so friendly and helpful.

Traveling Abroad

Traveling can teach you the ins and outs of being in a different city, state, or country. You may need to change currency or go to a bank to get larger or smaller bills. But through it all, you will learn how to get around and navigate how to communicate even when you do not speak the language.

My first trip to Europe took a bit of planning. I loved that I could go explore whatever I wanted. Music, museums, and shops were at my fingertips. I met some people working in the London office of the same organization I volunteered for in San Francisco. It was amazing how easy it was, through this common thread, to become friends. They took me around; I was intrigued by some of the different traditions, such as afternoon tea, and how different the food was from American food. I was amazed at how fashionably dressed many people were and how many businesses were furnished with antiques!

I went back to Europe many times and made friends in several countries, particularly Spain, Portugal, and Morocco. Whenever I returned, I knew I had a place to stay.

Getting to know people in different countries helps broaden your network. Meeting people throughout the world can create long-term relationships, whether for business or friendship.

When going abroad, you'll feel empowered by staying on your own, going to eat when you want, starting your day when you want, and enjoying being self-reliant. That being said, it is also wonderful to make friends that you can stay with. Plus it's cheaper, and they know the area.

When facing challenging situations like missing a plane, negotiating prices for purchases, knowing the route on the subway or bus, or communicating in a different language, you practice your problem-solving skills and expand your self-confidence.

Traveling also helps you to understand world issues. In some areas, you may get a glimpse at a nation's politics. You may also notice obvious cultural differences within the same country or experience innovations not used in your country. You might even see firsthand how climate issues are affecting the area you are visiting.

When you travel, you broaden your perspective and develop an understanding of different cultures. You have an opportunity to try different foods, have conversations with people with different histories, explore different geographical settings, and experience sights that are new and unusual to what you have experienced. This will make you very interesting at dinner parties and on social media!

How to Start Traveling

I recommend that people travel as soon as they can. I found traveling to be among life's most enriching experiences. I gained a perspective on different cultures, religions, and traditions. Travel has made me more empathetic to the struggles of people from different lands.

Sometimes young adults can find exchange programs, study scholarships, internships, or jobs that pay or help cover expenses for travel—sometimes even living expenses.

Here are some tips that can make travel safer and easier for you:

- Study up on the area you will be visiting. Find a map of where you will be staying, especially in places with less reliable internet services.
- Be sure to apply for passports and visas many months before your trip. There is nothing worse than waiting for your papers to arrive right before your trip. Contact your local passport office to find out how much time you should allot from start to finish.
- Research the laws of your destination, as some countries have rules that could be problematic if you break them. In countries that do not have free speech, criticizing the government or a religion (even online) can get you arrested. Some countries have no tolerance for those who are intoxicated in public. Know the law to avoid getting picked up and jailed.
- In North Korea and Egypt, taking pictures of airports, military areas, and locals can cause the police to detain you or deport you. Learn the key customs and cultural differences you might face. Check to see if there are any travel advisories for the area you are planning to visit.
- Make a copy of your passport, ID, visa, travel and medical Insurance, travel itinerary, travel tickets, important phone numbers, names, and addresses, the phone number of the place you will be residing during your stay, and the number of your country's embassy.
- Keep your copies separate from the originals. Some like to store this information on their phone, saved in the cloud. Many people use fanny packs, money belts, or cross-body bags to store their important documents.
- Avoid standing out. Wear clothing that locals wear, and do not flash a bunch of money in public or wear expensive jewelry (leave this at home). Tourists can be a mark for thieves and scammers. Stay aware of what is happening around you.
- Have a phrase book handy to translate if needed. Load a translator app to your phone. Use Google Translate. If you have the time, take a class in the language of the locals.

- If you plan on driving in the country of your destination, learn what the driving laws are and apply for an international license. An International Driver's Permit is a translation of your US driver's license into at least ten different languages. You must also bring your valid US driver's license to use when driving in a foreign country. An international license is good for one year.

  You can get the International Driver's Permit from the American Automobile Association (www.aaa.com) or the American Automobile Touring Alliance (www.aataidp.com).

  To apply, go to the office in your area or apply by mail. You will need the following:

  » Your valid US driver's license
  » A completed application (download from the two websites listed above)
  » Two passport pictures
  » $20 (or around that amount)

  If you wish to rent a car, note that some countries have age minimums (twenty to twenty-five). You may be charged an extra fee if you are younger.

  Be sure to apply for your license at least six weeks before your trip.

- If taking public transportation, know the route you will be taking. If you take a taxi, make sure it is with a reputable company.
- Check with the airline to find out what size luggage can be taken onto the plane as a carry-on. Inquire about the weight and size limits for checking your luggage. If you don't know the baggage rules, you could be charged a hefty additional fee for oversized bags or over-the-limit bags. Make a list of items not allowed to bring on board and what you can check in.
- Plan what you need to take with you well in advance. Make a list of what you will need to make your stay comfortable. Research what the weather will be like when you arrive.
- Be sure to take a comfortable, sturdy pair of shoes. Bring a beach towel (or camping towel), flip-flops (or Crocs), and a swimsuit if you will be lounging by the water. Take sunscreen so as not to get an uncomfortable burn (this could put a damper on your plans). Bring a hat.

- Take a small first-aid kit with bandages and antiseptic ointment, triple antibiotic ointment, mosquito repellant, and a small bottle of acetaminophen. Bring a couple of packets of travel-size tissues. Make sure the liquid amounts are allowed if you plan to put them in your carry-on.
- Unless you are going to a remote area, it is usually possible to purchase things like shampoo, toothpaste, and other personal items on arrival at your destination.
- Be sure to bring your medical card if you have insurance. Check with your insurance company to see whether you have coverage throughout the US and internationally. If you don't have insurance, you can purchase a plan that will cover expenses during your trip. Travel insurance often will cover medical expenses, missing luggage, trip cancellation, and other losses. Here is a list of some of the travel insurance companies:
    » Faye Travel Insurance (www.withfaye.com)
    » Travelex Insurance Services (www.tavelexinsurance.com)
    » Generali Global Assistance (www.generalitravelinsurance.com)
    » Travel Guard (AIG Travel Insurance, www.travelguard.com)
    » Seven Corners (www.sevencorners.com)
- If you need to take prescribed medication during your trip, be sure to bring it in the original container with the original information printed on the container by the pharmacy. It is also a good idea to bring a doctor's prescription slip for each medication you take, in case your stay is extended. You can also make a copy of your prescriptions on your phone. This assures you will be able to obtain a refill if you run out.
- Do not—I repeat, do not—bring drugs that are not prescribed for you. Aspirin, Tylenol, or other over-the-counter medications are OK. Never bring anything considered illegal. Marijuana is not permitted in many countries. Do not attempt to purchase drugs when you are abroad. In some countries, the laws are very strict, and if arrested, you could spend several years in prison for an offense. If you are so inclined, enjoy an adult beverage instead.
- Keep your phone charged. Bring an international adapter if needed. Make sure you have international service. Leave your itinerary information with family and

friends. Make sure they have the number for where you are staying. Keep in contact, and agree to regular times you will call. If your plans change, let your family know.
- Do all the same things you do when at home to stay safe. Don't give out personal information, such as where you are staying. Keep alert. Do not accept drinks, rides, or food from strangers. Use your best judgment when meeting new people. Enjoy yourself, be friendly, but do it with some caution.

This sounds like a long list, but it is the best way to feel comfortable in an environment you are not familiar with. Follow the suggestions and enjoy your trip. New food, landmarks, and sights await. Bon voyage!

CHAPTER 9
Creativity

Creativity can be satisfying and add to your sense of well-being. It is important for your cognitive function, creative self-expression, and spatial perception. When you are creative, you stimulate areas of your brain that deal with problem-solving and expression. It also helps your body to release dopamine, which can reduce stress, increase productivity, and improve your critical thinking.

Staying creative can improve cognitive function throughout your life. It may reduce the decline in brain function as you age, keeping your mind challenged and active.

Creativity allows you to experiment and embrace new experiences. This can help you learn new ways to adapt. Creativity does not necessarily have to be limited to the typical areas of artistic modes (dance, music, visual art, creative writing, film-making, sculpting, etc.). It can also include problem-solving, interior design, cooking, engineering design, architecture, inventing, and more.

I have had many creative outlets in my life, starting with making collages as a young child. My haven was my bedroom, where my imagination had free rein. At the same time, I enjoyed putting on my tutu and dancing around the house as if I were a ballerina. This turned into a lifetime of creative expression including singing, songwriting, dance, jewelry creation, writing, and paper arts. It took some time to develop skills and abilities in each area, and I found the learning and mentoring I received to be very important. The support I received spurred me to look beyond my own perception and recognize how I might be limiting myself. I learned through others sharing their techniques, philosophies, and viewpoints.

So How Do You Become Creative?

Creativity occurs when you use your imagination to develop a unique expression of yourself. It can be a means to set yourself apart from others by identifying how you define yourself. But at its core, creativity is about experimenting—trying things out and being flexible. You may use your manner of dress, digital content on social media, or your verbal manner to highlight who you are. It could also be through playing an instrument or joining a group that discusses solutions to issues.

To harness your creativity, do not be afraid to try new things. Creativity can be learned, and if you don't like the results at first, remember that everyone starts out in the same place, wherever they are, and can learn from there. Allow yourself to explore your interests. Don't avoid an experience due to fear of making a mistake. Give yourself permission to try it out with the idea of self-expression in mind. Have fun!

Small steps can lead to enjoyable discoveries. Try rearranging your bedroom, cooking a new dish, writing in a journal, or decorating for a special occasion. Read a book or see a movie, choosing a genre you typically don't watch. Be creative and think beyond your norm.

The golden rule: Make it fun! Invite friends over to paint together, do karaoke, or join a writing group or a book club. Go to a dance class or a trivia night. Let yourself go. Get into the process, becoming aware of how you feel during the creative activity. Be mindful that you are exploring.

Some of us have vivid images that come out of our imaginations. Some of us learn a skill, such as pottery, and then the vision occurs. Great works come from either place. Your goal in developing as a creative person is to find some way to express your thoughts and feelings, realizing your vision. How this turns into art is mostly an experiment. Take risks and develop a lifelong love of creating!

Famous Creators Through the Centuries

To get you started, here are some of the processes that famous creators used through the centuries:

Painters

Michelangelo Di Lodovico Buonarroti Simoni

Born March 6, 1475, died February 18, 1564

Michelangelo was born in the Florentine Republic of Italy. He was a painter, a poet, a sculptor, and an architect during the Renaissance period. Due to his prodigious skills, the term *renaissance man* became a popular term that is still used today to define a person who has many creative abilities.

Michelangelo showed great talent for drawing at an early age. His drawings often depicted the human form in detail. He was exposed, starting in his early teens, to numerous creative masters. Florence (where he grew up) was known for being a creative hub. He began studies in fresco painting (painting on wet plastered walls with powdered pigments), sculpture (he often worked in marble), and architecture, becoming a master in those areas. He created the famous statue *David* and the fresco of *The Creation of Adam* on the ceiling of the Sistine Chapel (Vatican City). Can you believe one guy did all of that!

Michelangelo believed his art was his way to connect with the divine nature of creativity. He found beauty in what he called "God's perfect creations." Through his artistry, he felt he was bringing spirituality to life.

Andy Warhol (Andrew Whahola Jr.)

Born August 6, 1928, died February 22, 1987

Born in Pittsburg, Pennsylvania, Andy Warhol was one of a group of artists who started the pop art movement. The movement often focused on popular objects. Warhol was known for his *Campbell's Soup Cans* and his depiction of Marilyn Monroe. His prints, photographs, and paintings embodied pop culture at the time.

Growing up, he had health issues and frequently was bedridden. This gave Andy time to look through his mother's magazine collection, which is how he developed skills in drawing. He also was very interested in Hollywood stars, and he began to couple his artwork with stories about them.

As a young man, he studied commercial art and moved to New York City to work as an illustrator for advertisements. This led him to printing and mass media. He became interested in how everyday objects and day-to-day life could be depicted in this new modern world. The rapid, busy life of celebrities and how they were then portrayed in the media fascinated him. He began to see that through art and creativity, he could alter people's perceptions. His work expanded to collaboration with other artists in his studio called the Factory.

Warhol bucked convention and used a certain amount of detachment to portray his message. He purposely stayed away from interjecting emotion into his work, thereby redefining the concept of art.

Salvador Dali (Salvador Domingo Felipe Jacinto Dali Domenech)

Born May 11, 1904, died January 23, 1989

Salvador Dali was from Figueres, Spain. At an early age, he studied the classic artists of the Renaissance period and the impressionists. In 1929, Dali joined the Surrealist movement, which was characterized by dreamlike paintings based on fantasies. His art juxtaposes seemingly random objects: a chair in the desert and a melting clock with a strange unrealistic animal standing beside it. These images were often derived from mythological or psychological symbols.

The Surrealists were a like-minded group. They welcomed Dali's addition of realism to the Surrealist goal of expanding one's imagination to depict deep dreamlike states.

The work of Sigmund Freud influenced Dali's images. He studied Freud's psychoanalytic theories of the unconscious mind, the interpretation of dreams, and the repression of desire. Many considered his paintings to be bizarre or strangely whimsical. He attempted to contrast that which is conscious with the dreamlike state of the unconscious.

Salvador merged aspects of psychoanalytic theory, mysticism, science, religion, and philosophy to create scenes that were meant to spark his viewers to look, question, and interpret for themselves the odd images he brought forth.

Dali used images that appeared to be melting, isolated, secured to the ground, mystical, dead, and often set against desert like scenery.

He was known as an eccentric individual. He often wore outlandish clothes. One of his signature looks was his notable stringlike, thin mustache, which he waxed to point the ends upward.

He was friends with fashion designers, other artists, filmmakers, and almost anyone who enjoyed his antics. He often drew an entourage of people around him eager to see what mischief he was up to.

Jean-Michel Basquiat

Born December 22, 1960, died August 12, 1988

Jean-Michel grew up in Brooklyn, New York, where his mother encouraged him to expand his artistic abilities. She would take him to art museums and galleries, developing his keen interest in drawing and the various modes of art.

As a teen, he noticed the artwork on buildings as he traveled around the city. With a friend, he formed a graffiti art duo SAMO (which meant Same Old S--t). This led him to enter the underground art scene. He was fascinated by the uninhibited style of expression of graffiti artists. Intrigued by symbols and spurred to learn new languages, he began to use diagrams and text in a manner that pointed out the contrast in the society he saw around him. These areas included themes such as self-identity, racial disparities, economic differences, and power. Being of Puerto Rican and Haitian heritage, his art evokes his feelings about the marginalization of Black artists.

In the late 1970s, Basquiat entered the New York art scene, where he socialized with artists like Andy Warhol and Kieth Harding. His art transitioned from streets to galleries that housed the latest trending artists.

He began to mix numerous styles of painting using bright colors with words and figures in an abstract manner. Basquiat used his art to express his own struggles in life. At times he expressed his inner turmoil using dark bold strokes with cubist figures.

He rose to fame, becoming one of the youngest artists to show in numerous exhibits and galleries. Some of his paintings sold for millions of dollars! Unfortunately, money is not everything. He struggled with mental health issues and succumbed to an overdose of drugs at the age of twenty-seven. It was a great loss to the art community and to those who found solace and representation in his art.

Peter Max Finkelstein

Born October 19, 1937

Peter Max was born in Berlin, Germany. His parents fled the area during the Nazi occupation. They settled in Shanghai, China for ten years and then moved to Israel, France, and the United States.

Due to his exposure to several cultures, he picked up artistic styles and colors that represented these varied ways of life. In his youth, he became enamored with the cosmos. Themes involving space became recurring images in his paintings.

He took classes at the Louvre and discovered a style of painting called Fauvism. The artwork was colorful, sometimes including brush strokes with free movements. Henri Matisse was a good example of an artist who used this style. Peter Max continued his studies in painting, figure drawing, and anatomy at the Art Students League of New York.

During the 1960s, his work encompassed bright colors, pop-art ideology, and surreal visions brought about by the psychedelic movement.

While establishing himself, he started a studio with two of his friends, and they received acknowledgment for their accomplishments together. Later he moved on to advertising and commercial art, which included work on album covers and posters. He became a 1960s icon.

His artwork inspired happiness. People often regarded it as having come from colorful fantasies. He also painted president's portraits, paintings of the Beatles, and even portraits of Taylor Swift.

His work was used in materials that supported environmental issues and activities promoting peace. He often focused on images that expressed his spirituality and his feelings of being at one with the world. He incorporated his interest in Eastern philosophy and his wish for unity. He was aligned with the counterculture of the time.

Architects

Julia Morgan

Born January 20, 1872, died February 2, 1957

Julia Morgan was born in San Francisco, California. As a youngster Julia enjoyed mathematics. Later she studied in the Engineering Department at the University of California in Berkeley. Often, she found that she was the only female in the classes that related to her major. In her early college years, she helped to establish the first local YWCA. She was the first woman to graduate with a BA in engineering at the university and received honors and accolades for her feat.

While at a lecture in college, Morgan met the famous architect, Bernard Maybeck, and joined his architecture group. She admired his ability to utilize the natural world in his designs, and he became one of her most influential mentors. He encouraged her to go to the renowned Ecole des Beaux-Arts in Paris. Morgan became the first female to earn a certificate of architecture at the school. A pioneer throughout her life, she paved the way for women to participate in activities that were previously closed to them.

Her buildings were structurally strong. She enjoyed working with clients to create inspiring designs that incorporated Mission Revival styles, Mediterranean motifs, and arts and crafts themes. She used the landscapes to keep the natural feel of the surroundings.

She created hundreds of buildings, including Mills College in Oakland, California, several YWCAs throughout the country, the Asilomar Conference Center in California, and the Hearst Castle project in San Simeon, California—just to name a few of her well-known projects.

Julia Morgan was a strong, independent woman. She strived to be self-sufficient, not taking any funds from her wealthy family. She was inducted into the California Hall of Fame in 2008 after her death.

Bjarke Ingels

Born October 2, 1974

Bjarke Ingels was born in Copenhagen, Denmark. Initially he was interested in using drawing, through cartooning, to tell stories. He eventually was drawn to architecture and attended the Royal Danish Academy, also in Copenhagen. He went on to study in Barcelona, Spain, at the Escola Technica Superior d'Arquitectura. While living in Spain, he became enamored with Antonio Gaudí's whimsical architectural style depicting swirls, waves, and other organic motifs. Ingel's visions of design were progressive and unconventional. He began to look for both utility and sustainability in his projects.

He collaborated with other architects, and he started to think in terms of the environment. Bjarke began to impact people by designing structures for living. He took into consideration their work, social, and recreational needs.

Ingels founded the Bjarke Ingels Group, a worldwide company that employs over seven hundred people. He valued teamwork and sharing ideas and perspectives. This became a driving philosophy for the growth of his company. Many of his designs have gained worldwide acclaim including *Mountain Dwellings,* the 8 House housing complex, and the California Google North Bayshore Headquarters. His buildings are carefully engineered, modern artistic masterpieces. His company has won a multitude of awards for design and structure. They even worked with Lego to develop the Lego House. So far, the company has worked on a dizzying number of projects in numerous countries.

Antonio Gaudí (I Cornet)

Born June 25, 1852, died June 10, 1926

Gaudí was born in Reus (or possibly Riudoms), Catalonia, Spain. He was ill throughout his childhood and suffered from rheumatism (a chronic disease that can affect the bones, kidneys, joints, heart, and lungs). Because of his ailment, he often spent time at home drawing and exploring nature. This led to his use of living things around him in his designs.

He grew up in a family of artists (coppersmiths). Their use of precision in their designs and their use of tools to create intricate patterns greatly influenced him, as seen in his various depictions of waves, animals, trees, shell spirals, and flowers.

As a young man, Gaudí's Catholic religion became more and more meaningful to him. Intertwined with this was his interest in utopian socialism, a perspective that envisioned fantasy societies where people could live in harmony.

In 1875 he served in mandatory military service in Barcelona. Due to his chronic health condition, he was put on sick leave and returned to study architecture. He paid for his schooling by becoming an engineering technician, making technical drawings for architects, eventually receiving an architectural degree from the Barcelona Architecture School.

One of his first projects was the Casa Vicens, built from 1883 to 1885. Although this building was considered part of his orientalist period, it was one of the first of his buildings to embody modernism.

He created many delightful buildings, often featuring colorful mosaics or ceramic features. Some of his buildings had wavelike peaks and interesting balconies. His churches were elaborate and detailed—true works of art. He felt he was inspired to create buildings that celebrated his devotion to God.

Gaudí died at the age of seventy-three, after injuries sustained from a passing tram.

Music

Yo-Yo Ma

Born October 7, 1955

Yo-Yo Ma was born in Paris, France. He began his musical studies at the age of four and was considered a child prodigy. Both of his parents were accomplished musicians from China who instilled in him a deep admiration for music. He was encouraged to spend a good amount of time practicing cello, and during his childhood, he had numerous performances both on television and with well-known musicians. Through his early dedication to his music, he positioned himself to become a sought-after student.

His family eventually moved to New York City. Yo-Yo Ma was technically astute by the time he entered the Juilliard School. He then moved on to the professional Children's School, graduating at the age of fifteen. He started at Harvard after he had a multitude of experiences performing with masters. He studied anthropology, becoming interested in the relationship between music and culture. Later in life, Harvard awarded him an honorary doctorate.

He played with musicians from various genres, from classical to jazz to rock to Brazilian music and everything in between. His vast experience allowed Yo-Yo Ma to work with masters from many countries using intriguing styles of music and unusual instruments.

Yo-Yo Ma believes that continual practice, taking on challenges, and ongoing self-expansion—including being curious, developing empathy, connecting with others through collaboration, and sharing innovative ideas—all add to one's creativity and understanding of music. He feels that music has the power to take people beyond their boundaries.

Recommended Listening Yo-Yo Ma (YouTube)

- "Over the Rainbow"
- Yo-Yo Ma and Stuart Duncan

@yoyoma (Instagram)

Ren (Eryn Gill)

Born March 29, 1990

Ren was born in Bangor, Gwynedd, Wales. At an early age, he became interested in creating music. His parents took him to concerts as a youngster, and he learned to play guitar by playing along with the music of Jimi Hendrix and others. When he created beats, he recorded them on CDs, then sold them. He also started to perform.

Ren went to Bath Spa University (Newton Park Campus) but began to experience health issues. He graduated with a Bachelor of Arts with honors in commercial music.

When he was able, he began busking (receiving donations from playing publicly, usually on the street). He played with a group called the Big Push.

His music drew crowds who were taken by his expertise. Ren was proficient in playing several instruments, and his vocal style ranged from rock, punk rock, and jazz. He used his vocal capabilities to do his own version of scat (using vocalizations to form notes that are not words but are sounds), and he also amazed people with his ability to tell stories through rap.

During this time, he was noticed by a music producer, who signed him to his label. This is where Ren's career started to take off. He worked with a variety of people and got notice and airtime. Videos of his songs ignited a phenomenal word-of-mouth fan base that made his music viral.

While on tour, he fell ill and ended up being bedridden for many months. During this time, he was misdiagnosed multiple times and was treated with medication that seemed to make him feel worse.

On October 20, 2023, Ren gained the number-one spot in the UK Official Albums Chart for his album *Sic Boi*. He has become an advocate for developing means to deal with long-term illness and mental health care and awareness.

Ren focuses his song "Sic Boi" on his journey with his illness, from being constantly in pain, feeling betrayed by the medical field, and having suicidal thoughts.

His decision to get intensive help at a hospital in Canada allowed him to adapt to a healthier lifestyle and gain mental stability. He was diagnosed with Lyme disease and mast cell activation disorder.

As of late, he has been quite prolific in his music endeavors, creating one thought-provoking and deeply moving piece after another. Each creation is excellent. He moves way beyond anything mundane. He slaps us awake with the depth of the stories he tells in his songs.

Recommended Listening: Ren (YouTube)

- "Sick Boi"
- "Hi Ren"
- "Slaughterhouse"
- "Money Ties"

@Renmakesmusic (Instagram)

Shara Nova

Born April 22, 1974

Shara was born in El Dorado, Arkansas, to parents who both were involved in music through their church. Shara also sang in church and learned piano from her uncle, a jazz and classical pianist. In her adolescence, she listened to famous operatic singers and loved the theatrical aspect of opera, driving her to study classical singing and composition at the University of North Texas. While studying Russian in Moscow, she produced her first recording.

After her immersive operatic studies, she became an astute vocalist. She moved to New York, New York, excited to explore the burgeoning music scene. During this time, she encountered experimental music and was mentored by operatic singer Josephine Mongiardo, with other mentors to follow.

In 2006, she released the album *Bring Me the Workhorse* under the name My Brightest Diamond. Using this name, she produced numerous EPs, remixes, and singles. She appears onstage, often with a fiery red head of hair, a guitar, and interesting clothes. The contrast between her beautiful, classically trained voice and the indie-rock and electronic music that accompanies her is unexpected but mesmerizing.

Shara has strived to blend music genres, to work on projects that are both challenging and satisfying, and to connect with creatives to express her feelings and ideas about the human experience. She feels that music can be transformative and allow for vulnerability.

Shara's experience is broad. Her musical offerings are current and often relevant to the issues of today. Her dedication and expertise have brought her to leading orchestras, writing music for others, collaborating with many well-known people, directing productions, mentoring young musicians, writing operas, and producing and recording her own music.

Hers is a journey still in progress. Her early encouragement, continued training, and passion for experiencing her work on a very personal level have brought her to a place of great success.

Recommended Listening: Shara Nova (YouTube)

- "Hymns for Private Use"
- "My Brightest Diamond" (Shara Nova's Group)
- "Rising Star"
- "It's Me On the Dance Floor"

Ending Thoughts About Creativity

Creativity comes in many forms. Imagination may be expressed in a multitude of areas. Writers, poets, dancers, woodworkers, glass artists, engineers, and interior decorators are a few more types of creators. Some artists have been self-taught, and others have had formal training. Numerous artists have found a means to express their difficulties, override the limits of illness, and engage others in their stories through art.

These artists all brought their dreams and philosophies into their works. Each is unique because of their own perceptions and feelings about life. Some of them portray life darkly, others depict their religious beliefs, while others infuse their art with whimsy and dreamlike images.

However you come to self-expression, it can be a fulfilling aspect of your individualism, sharing who you are through an art form. Take a few moments and list the artistic activities that you really like to participate in. Then ask yourself what would happen if you took that passion further. What would be the next step for you? Let yourself explore that creative process. Find something that will engage you and bring some expressive satisfaction.

CHAPTER 10

Prioritizing for Round-the-Clock Success

Managing time is the key to getting projects done, showing up on time, and getting enough sleep. It's a requirement if you want to eat a healthy meal, exercise, take your dog out for a walk, visit with friends, and finish work. Whether it's for a job, or it's homework for a class, or it's housecleaning, being in control of the clock is a necessity for reaching your goals.

Procrastination

Most people have experienced procrastination at times throughout their life. You know, the times when you find just about anything else to do, except the project you set out to work on.

There are many reasons for such behavior. Here is a list of contributing issues:

- **Self-Doubt.** Clouding your view of yourself with negative thoughts like "Can I really do this?" or "I don't know if I can figure out where to start."
- **Fear of Failure.** Not taking on a project so that you avoid dealing with the potential that you will not succeed.
- **Lack of Inspiration.** Not having the motivation to begin or complete the task.
- **Looming Stressors.** Feeling anxiety about taking on a large project or uncertainty about how to organize it.
- **Perfectionism.** Feeling as if every little detail must be in place before you start. You set unreasonable expectations before allowing yourself to finish.
- **Getting Distracted.** Social media, television, and phone calls can distract you from getting things done. Also, having an environment that is disorganized, noisy, or cluttered can keep you from focusing on other tasks.
- **Not Using Time Well.** Not leaving enough time to get the job done and not prioritizing what is most important.

- **No Accountability.** Not holding yourself responsible for getting something completed. You have not set up an accountability system where you have a friend, family member, or work buddy to hold you responsible for what you need to get done.
- **Avoidance.** Avoiding tasks when labeling them as boring, too hard, or uncomfortable to do, such as putting off laundry for a week even though you have no socks to wear or not making an appointment with the doctor because you wish to avoid an uncomfortable situation (even though you are in pain).
- **Not Up to It.** You may not be getting enough sleep, or you may feel sick or are having mental health issues. Examine what is causing your issues and seek medical help if this slump persists.
- **Resistant to Authority.** You see chores or deadlines as external demands when the pressure actually comes from within. Often people react to a struggle between their independence and what they see as a takeover of their time from tasks demanding their attention.

Go over the modes of procrastination as outlined above. Write which of the modes affects you the most. After each mode, write down things that can help you to avoid putting things off.

- Consider keeping an appointment book or digital detailing of what you need to do. There is a saying that once you write something down, it makes it real. I use my Alexa device to remind me of classes coming up, Zoom meetings, deadlines for bills, and so on. It helps to keep me on track.
- Sometimes you need an accountability partner—someone you can tell what you are doing and will be there to support you to get it done. Train yourself to follow through if you tell someone you will have a project ready for them at a certain time.
- If you commit to doing something you don't want to do, understand why you are resisting it. Maybe you're taking on something you haven't done before—going with a friend to ballroom dancing, let's say. Talk about it with the friend. See if you can have some resolution to your feelings and try something new!

- Don't commit to so many things that you overwhelm yourself. Know your schedule and what can reasonably get done in the time you have.

In the next section, we will look at how to set goals. This is an important step to getting clear enough to get started and have an understanding of where you are headed.

Goal Setting

Setting goals can be the key to avoiding procrastination. Holding yourself responsible for completing a task is an end goal. Setting a target helps you to be clear about what you want to focus on. A detailed goal can help you to monitor your progress and feel good about your movement toward completion.

What are your goals in the following areas?

- **Career Goals**
  Examples: Learn to use AI, get an internship, learn how to get a small business loan, or find a job in another city.
- **Education**
  Examples: Take an online class, get my bachelor of arts degree, learn a new language, or start a study group.
- **Finances**
  Examples: Open a savings account, learn about the stock market and investing, or set up an automatic deposit of $200 monthly to my money market account.
- **Relationships**
  Examples: See family members more often, make some new friends, or start dating again.
- **Self-Development**
  Examples: Try something new to build self-esteem, go on a trip alone, or join a book club.
- **Health**
  Examples: Join a fitness club, get new glasses, or start seeing a therapist.

SMART Goals System

This system was originally introduced by George T. Duran in 1981. Since then, his system has been used frequently in the fields of business, project management, education, self-development, and training. Use this to set up an outline for your goal (example below):

- **S** = *Specific*. Define your goal and how you will meet it.
- **M** = *Measurable*. How will you measure the progress?
- **A** = *Achievable*. Is this doable?
- **R** = *Relevant*. Does this fit with your use of time and interests? Is this a task that is required or that will help your life?
- **T** = *Time Bound*. What is the timeline to get this finished?

Example

Specific

My *specific* goal is to learn how to dye fabric using natural plant dyes fabric. I will take an online course. I will learn how to prepare the fabric to take the dye. I will learn how to select plants that will impart a dye to the fabric. I will learn whether a final rinse is needed to help hold in the dye. I will keep a notebook of relevant notes on the processes. When done with the class, I will practice. My end goal is to make eight T-shirts for my volunteers.

Measurable

I will *measure* my progress by keeping a notebook and writing down any questions I must ask the instructor before we start the next day. As I learn each aspect of the process, I will write down what I have learned from the class that day.

Achievable

This goal is *achievable*. I will attend all four classes, take good notes, and practice after the class.

Relevant

Yes, this project is *relevant*. When finished, I will have made eight T-shirts to give to the eight girls who volunteered for the recent park clean-up day.

Time Bound

Here is my *timeline*. I will attend the online class from May 1 through May 4. I will have more than three weeks to practice and create the T-shirts. I will meet with the girls for a group picnic with staff on May 29. On that day, I will have the shirts ready to hand out to the girls.

Your Goal Outline

Now it is your turn to pick a goal to achieve. Pick something that you are just starting on or something that you wish to get started. Use the SMART goal system above to help you write a clear goal for yourself. Then follow through. You can write in your notebook what was easy about this exercise, what was hard, and what you can do to keep on track.

S -

M -

A -

R -

T -

Now that you know the system, let's find out what goals are really important to you.

Exercise

Here is an exercise that can assist you in pinpointing what is most important to you. Take a sheet of paper and fold it lengthwise in half. Label one column "Long-Term Goals" and one column "Short-Term Goals."

Long-Term Goals	**Short-Term Goals**
Visit the Smithsonian	Get a new haircut style
Learn to do artwork with AI	Celebrate parent's anniversary
Save for tickets to go to NY	Build three raised beds
Join a gym to get fit	Plant veggie and flower seeds
Take a writing class	Bake bread for a potluck

Now you have identified your goals and have written them down.

The next important step is to figure out how to schedule your life so that the goals and plans you have can happen.

Knowing how much time you need to spend on each task helps you to plan your day, week, and month. The first thing to do is designate which activities are urgent, occurring weekly, flexible, or something that happens in the future. This allows you to be accountable, to not feel overwhelmed, and to feel in control of the things you want to accomplish.

Here is an example of how you can make a chart to help you with task management.

Task	Priority	Time
Grocery Shopping	MI	1.5 hours
Call Mom/Dad	MI	30 minutes
Water Plants	W	30 minutes
Wash Laundry	W	3 hours
Dentist Appointment	FG	2 hours
Read 3 new books	FG	4 hours per week
Walk dog	MI	45 minutes
Date night	FG	3 hours

Key to Abbreviations for Task Management

- **Future Goal (FG) -** Tasks set for long-term achievements
- **Weekly (W) -** Routine tasks that need to be done every week
- **Most Important (MI) -** High priority tasks that need immediate attention
- **Least Important (LI) -** Tasks that can be done when time permits
- **Monthly Tasks (MT) -** Tasks to be accomplished within the month
- **Current Goals (CG) -** Short-term goals that are in progress

I have an appointment book that I write my daily schedule in (some people use their electronic devices). It's important to write down what you have committed to each week, including chores. This helps you to develop a routine. Taking charge of your time allows you to master the art of prioritizing and managing tasks.

CHAPTER 11
Government

The world is changing—fast. The early 2000s look stagnant in comparison! All at once, we're experiencing major changes to government, politics, business, entrepreneurship, and technology. We are on the verge of a metamorphosis, putting our entire governmental structure in flux.

It is important to understand how the government works. This will allow you to make decisions for your own future by picking representatives who will reflect your ideals and ensure that all constituents have a voice.

It is easy for some government officials to be short-sighted and only stand for what they perceive is important. Contact your representatives with concerns you may have, such as about veteran's affairs, pollution, rising crime, education, and so on. Take your right to vote seriously and find out who the candidates are. Go to town hall meetings, write letters to representatives, and get involved.

Government plays a pivotal role in determining the direction we go as a country. The importance of taking your stand as a voter is not only a right but also a statement of how you want to see your country represented in the world. This is a cornerstone of our democracy and Constitution.

The US government is made up of three branches.

Executive Branch

The president is the head of state, leader of the federal government, and commander in chief of the US armed forces. The executive branch implements and enforces laws. The vice president supports the president, presides over the US Senate, and breaks ties in Senate votes.

Cabinet members serve as advisers to the president. They include the vice president, heads of executive departments, and other high-ranking government officials.

Legislative Branch

This branch is made up of Congress, which has two chambers.

The upper chamber is known as the Senate. Two senators per state are chosen for a six-year term that is staggered every two years. Their duties consist of approving or rejecting presidential appointments to the executive branch, drafting proposed laws, sanctioning treaties with foreign countries, declaring war, and conducting impeachment trials.

The lower chamber of Congress is known as the House of Representatives, which has 435 members. Each state receives a certain number of members based on each state's population. Representatives serve two-year terms. Their special duties are to initiate revenue-raising bills and to impeach federal officials, such as the president.

Both the House and the Senate must agree on a bill before it passes. This can take many days as different sides argue, make compromises, re-draft bills, and work to get an agreement. If passed, the bill then goes to the president, who can veto or approve the bill. A two-thirds congressional vote can override a veto.

The idea of Congress is that each member represents a different area of the country, reflecting the ideals and different needs of their constituents.

Judicial Branch

This branch consists of the Supreme Court and other federal courts. The courts interpret the meaning of laws, apply laws to individual cases, and decide whether laws violate the Constitution.

Checks and Balances

Checks and balances are a system that is like a safety net. It is meant to keep any one branch of government from having too much power. Each branch has its own role. If one branch seems to step out of line, the other branches can call them out. For example, the president can veto laws suggested by the legislative branch, and Congress can override a veto if they have enough votes. The courts interpret laws, and they can rule that the actions taken are unconstitutional. They can then block those laws that have been passed. This system offers a way to honor and protect people's rights according to what is written in the Constitution. It allows people to have a way to voice concerns and hold leaders accountable. Understanding this helps you to recognize whether our government is working or moving away from what values the country was founded upon.

The Popular Vote

You may have heard the phrase, *Your vote is your voice.* Every valid ballot is expected to be turned in and counted. Counting ballots is a process where verification and multiple checks for accuracy are taken very seriously. There are different types of voting processes: early voting, provisional ballots, mail-in ballots, and Election Day ballots. These types of ballots can all have different deadline dates to afford time for election officials to process them, including the verification of addresses or to resolve discrepancies that are discovered. All votes are recorded and carefully supervised. All candidate races (except the president and the vice president) are decided through a popular vote.

The Electoral College

The United States uses a system called the Electoral College to elect the president and vice president. Even the founding fathers of our country—the signers of the Declaration of Independence and writers of the Constitution—were split on deciding what was the best method to elect the two top people in our government. Some felt that it should be decided by the people's vote. Another group thought the parties should select chosen electors that would be the representatives of the winner. As a compromise, they decided to have a popular vote and then a vote by the electors to vote their parties' slate. They believed this would fairly balance the distribution of power.

To this day, the Electoral College system is controversial. Many voters feel it should be abolished. They believe that election results should be based purely on the idea that the most votes received per candidate will be named the winner.

What Is the Electoral College?

Every four years, a group of presidential electors is chosen for the sole purpose of electing the president and vice president. The number of electoral votes for each state is determined by the number of senators (two) plus the number of representatives for that state. The number of representatives varies by the population of each state. For instance, the large state of California has fifty-three electors, while the smaller state of Hawaii has four electors.

The political parties (Democrats and Republicans) of each state select a slate of electors—a group of politically minded persons pledging to vote for that party's candidate. These electors are loyal party members of their party. Each party gets equal electors per state. Washington, DC, and forty-eight states are considered winner-take-all states. The winning candidate must have 51 percent of the vote. They then receive all the electoral votes for that state.

Has the Electoral College Become an Outdated System?

Only 40 percent of Americans understand what the Electoral College is. Many voters dislike that a candidate can win the popular vote but lose the election because of the Electoral College vote. This system causes candidates to focus more of their attention on contested battleground states (states that can go to either party), meaning they spend less time campaigning in the states where they have strong followings or in states where they are not popular candidates. Finally, electors can change their vote.

There is another system that operates in Nebraska and Maine. They use a system called the district method. Here, each state has two statewide electors (one for each senator) and one elector for each congressional district. Sometimes these votes can be for two different parties.

Understanding how government works is not only for politicians or political pundits (a person who knows a lot about a subject and gives information or opinions about it)—it is important for anyone who wants a say in our country. The government shapes everything from the laws that govern you to the services they provide, the taxes you pay, and the infrastructure for roads and highways. You can make informed decisions when you understand how it works. You can then ask questions of your officials, decide how you wish to vote, and be involved in making your community or state better. You can stay informed, advocate for things that are important to you, and possibly run for office.

It is both your responsibility and your right to stand up for what occurs in your future! Don't give that power away.

CHAPTER 12
Politics

Did you know that there are more than two parties in America?

There are some third groups such as the Libertarians, the Green Party, the Reform Party, and the Constitution Party, which have had a minor showing of voters. Some have made a small dent in catching votes, but most of these groups have not had enough party participants to move the needle far at election time. Consequently, our politics operates more like a two-party system, and over the last decade, a previously congenial group of politicians and voters has become greatly divided.

I remember being a child when I first noticed the program *Meet the Press*. My father would watch it every week. Even though I probably would have rather watched cartoons, I sat attentively, trying to do my best to make sense of it. I waited until the end and then asked my questions. After a few sessions of watching the program, I was hooked. I didn't understand everything in depth until I was a teenager, but I always saw so much of life in those programs. It wasn't just life here. It was Russia, France, Vietnam, Germany, Bosnia, and many other countries. I learned there were issues occurring all over the world.

Whole groups of people were starving. It was a time of famine. AIDS was running rampant. Women were demanding rights and equal pay. I learned about civic engagement and started to volunteer at various places. During college, through one of my classes, I became a volunteer in a program for autistic children. I found a good fit, advocating for people.

Understanding the dynamics of politics can be like unraveling chains that have become entangled. There are areas you will agree upon, while other ideas may not fit your perspective. Through it all, listen to other people's points of view. Share your views and agree to listen to others. I have good friends who have different political views, but we still have a good amount of things in common.

Have you considered practicing civic engagement? Have you given thought to which political ideologies interest you? What ideas could you possibly advocate for? Perhaps you might be interested in health care and wish to work to acknowledge nurses who gave their time during the pandemic. Or perhaps you are interested in economic issues that may affect you as a young adult. Maybe you are a hiker or outdoor enthusiast, wanting to get involved with one of the many initiatives about environmental protection. There are many topics to explore and many ways to be an advocate. Get involved. Civic engagement feels good. It is a way to stand up for issues that you strongly care about.

CHAPTER 13

Finding a Job

Looking for a job can seem like a vast undertaking. Finding a position, whether it is your first job or your fifth, may leave you scratching your head.

Jobs are not merely a means to make money. They also allow you to build skills, get experience, and build a network. You don't have to get the perfect dream job, but it is important that there is something of value that you can learn from your position. Jobs may be a bridge to moving toward the occupation you would like as an outcome.

Since the application and interview process can take time, bolster your skills. Keep your confidence high. Be patient and give time for the process to evolve.

Receiving rejection notices is part of the process. By no means is this an indication that you are not valuable. There are many reasons that could explain why you were not picked. Do not dwell on this; rather, look to approach your next opportunity.

Clarify what type of job you feel you would especially thrive in. Examine what skills you have and how you could apply them to a work situation.

Maybe you would like a full-time job during the summer but a part-time job while you finish up your last year at college. Let's say that you've worked at a newspaper for two years handling calls and proofreading ads. With an interest in writing, you decide that eventually you would like to go into journalism. Think about what steps you would need to take to arrive at that outcome. You might look into going for a master's degree in journalism or writing freelance for local publications.

Have a plan but approach it with flexibility. Take into consideration your salary needs, lifestyle, and future objectives.

Be on the watch for scammers. Usually they have ads that offer spectacular things: your own car to use, six-figure salaries, travel to fully paid exotic paradises, and so on. It also is not a good idea to interview with a company that says there is a fee for training. Most reputable companies will pay for your training. Research the businesses that you apply to. Ask other people if they know of them.

Résumé

Writing a résumé can be a puzzling endeavor. Think of it as a glimpse into who you are. It gives the employer an impression of what you have to offer.

When writing your résumé, stay away from *I* and *My* and use phrases such as *full-time employee at Jake's Whole Foods* or *top buyer in the clothing department for three years*.

Your résumé should include:

- **Contact Information.** Include your full name, the address where you get your mail, your phone number, and your email.
- **A Summary.** Tell the employer about your experience. Be succinct and to the point. Usually a phrase for each listed item will do (e.g., *graduated with a master's degree in business, video editor with three years experience, managed a restaurant for two years, has strong management skills, excellent customer service skills,* or *works with and train teams*).
- **Your Computer Skills.** Are you computer literate in Microsoft Suite, Google Docs, Slack, Zoom, ChatGPT, Copilot AI, or Canva AI?
- **One Line About the Type of Job You Are Seeking.** This could include phrases like *seeks full-time work in marketing* or *seeks a management job with customer service*.
- **One Line About One of Your Achievements or Qualities.** Examples include *fluent in Spanish and Portuguese* and *received salesperson of the year award in 2024*.
- **Use Keywords From the Job Description.** For instance, if the job description says, "looking for an entry-level salesperson," include that exact wording in your résumé.

Here are several websites to visit for more information explaining how to lay out a résumé and what to include:

- www.resumegenius.com
- www.canva.com/resumes
- www.linkedin.com
- www.jobhero.com/resumesamples
- www.novoresume.com

Getting an Interview

Keep a log of when and to whom you send out your résumés. If you get called for an interview, also include that information in the log. I have heard of some companies taking a month before they interview candidates for a job.

Be prepared to have your interview by video, phone, or in person. If you will be doing an in-person or a video session, be sure to dress professionally. Practice using your phone in front of a mirror or with a friend.

An interview is a chance for you to highlight your skills and experience. Show interest and be enthusiastic about the meeting.

Send a thank-you note by email, acknowledging that you appreciate the opportunity to be interviewed. Comment that you are interested in the position.

If you have not heard back in a week or so, you can make contact again. Always be enthusiastic and gracious. This leaves the door open while they are making up their minds.

If you don't hear back, don't fret. This can happen for many reasons, and it may not have anything to do with you. Now is the time to use any feedback you have received to reevaluate your approach. Revise your résumé if needed. Expand the range of what you are applying for. Most people go through numerous interviews before they find the right fit. Do not give up—it's likely that a job for you is close on the horizon.

Mentors

Finding a mentor can be a very important aspect of your learning, training, or growth. A mentor usually helps in a specific area (such as how to work in a non-profit, or how to paint murals, or how to do research). They share their expertise and insight into their own journey to success, helping you to map out your own personal development. They can assist you to step over areas that they have found difficult, so that you can avoid similar failures. They can aid in acquiring new abilities and insights.

Mentors can often introduce you to other people doing similar work. Your mentor can aid in attaining networking and job opportunities. You may also meet colleagues and other professionals who are willing to share their experiences with you.

The mentor takes you under their wings and can make suggestions with your success in mind. By meeting with a mentor on a regular basis, you can learn to be accountable. Following through is an important aspect of becoming reliable. They can also help you to become self-assured through their encouragement.

I have had several mentors throughout my life. Each experience allowed me to gain confidence and expertise. One of the things I have carried with me is how grateful I am that my mentors took time to help me grow. In turn, I have mentored many people in the various areas I gained expertise in. It has been one of the most satisfying things I have done. I also have enjoyed lifelong friendships with some of my mentors and mentees.

How to find a mentor:

- Identify the area you wish to learn about.
- Talk to friends, family members, teachers and people in similar fields to see if they have recommendations for a person who could mentor you.
- Find a place to volunteer. You may meet people who would be interested to mentor you in a non-profit, business or any other location you are interested in.
- If you don't get any leads from them, research where the activity occurs in your area. Take down the contact information, think about how you wish to approach a potential mentor (call, send an email, send a letter by USPS). Ask if they have an opportunity to take on a mentee.
- If they do, make an appointment to meet. When you meet with them, explain why you wish to be mentored. Discuss the length of time you are willing to commit to. Explore how they would like to structure mentoring. Discuss what you hope to get out of the experience. If asked, discuss the value they could bring to your tutelage.

Take advantage of learning from someone who has already been there. Not only can you gain from their expertise, but you may also garner tips and support to enhance the skills you already have.

CHAPTER 14
Business and Entrepreneurship

I started selling my wares when I was in my teens. My high school friends liked the jewelry I made, and they would order specific earrings and bracelets to go with their outfits.

My first entrepreneurial adventure was making accessories for a New Wave clothes boutique. I made hand-dyed and -painted T-shirts with cool sayings on them with abstract designs, but my bread and butter was leather bandannas with studs and clasps. My first order was for 250 bandannas and forty shirts. I was so excited that the store was interested and that they made repeat orders. I got two more similar stores as customers, and for two years I was in the money! Eventually the New Wave style fizzled out. And thus, my first business ended.

I learned so much about marketing, customer relations, and procuring orders. After working for other people, I once again started a new business making jewelry from my torched-glass pendants and beads. I did that for nineteen years and moved on to taking a directorship at an arts council. I have always loved the challenge of exploring new opportunities and making a go with them.

With the advent of AI, there are opportunities to develop businesses with less start-up money, fewer employees, and accessible technology.

When thinking about starting your own business, you might be attracted to the perks: more freedom, more control, having a more flexible schedule, and making an impact on your community. You also might think making this leap is insurmountable.

But let's clear up some misconceptions about being an entrepreneur:

Myth	Reality
You need funds before you can start.	Many people start their businesses with minimal investments. Using crowdfunding, grants, or money from investors can give you a boost when starting out.
Entrepreneurs already have business skills.	A business degree is not required. Those who seek to create their own business have one thing in common: an idea they wish to develop into something all their own. The skills involved in running a business can be learned as you build your enterprise. Taking calculated risks, critical thinking, bookkeeping, developing products, developing good customer relations, and marketing are all things that can be learned.
You must have a unique product.	While some people start out with an idea of their own, many don't. My friend Jillian started a business doing hair color, cuts, and styling—and there were already many stylists in her community. But she managed to stand out in other ways. She created a unique modern environment. She had shelves to display local crafts and artwork. She offered coffee drinks and sparkling waters, and her waiting room consisted of café tables and chairs. People not only loved her expertise but loved that the environment was inviting and a great destination for finding gifts.
All entrepreneurs are always successful first try.	It's common for a business to begin one way but evolve into something else. Sometimes people need time to work out the kinks.

Mike was a creative baker. He started a specialized French bakery and catering business in 2019. He had specials every day and a large assortment of coffee drinks, teas, and freshly squeezed juices to accompany his baked goods.

He also had a delivery service and was popular with businesses with high-end clients and needs for service to large group meetings. He would do catering, complete with fruit platters, salads, eggs, fresh breads, store-made preserves, and cheese and meat platters. Then COVID came. Everything seemed to stop. He took a few weeks to think of what to do next.

He had to think his whole plan over again. While he was allowed to continue preparing food, he no longer was able to be open for customers. He hired more drivers, a few more kitchen staff members, someone to watch over computer orders and do billing, and someone to do phone orders and package food to go. He continued to cater but focused on orders by phone and drop-off delivery. He baked items and packaged them to sell in stores around town. Because he pivoted, he was able to maintain his business, even when his bakery had to close to walk-in customers.

He opened his doors after COVID. To his surprise, he had more customers and actually enlarged his space by taking over the small newspaper and bookstore that was next to him. He remodeled a bit and extended his hours for the lunch crowd. Again, he found his way to success.

What Mike did was to figure out how he could plan for the sustainability of his business. No one knew COVID was coming. He had to create a plan that could sustain him until he could resume his walk-in bakery business.

To be a successful business person, you have to be a problem solver. If you notice that something isn't working, try another way. Be creative in trying out fresh ideas. Examine trends such as AI. Use it in your business where it might help you move further.

Make It Work: Real Ways to Earn and Run a Business

There are many ways to do something you care about when it comes to making money. Whether you are offering a service, creating content, building a brand, or selling a product, tools exist to get started. Often you can learn business tips online or find programs at places like the Small Business Association or community colleges that offer free or inexpensive ways to get useful information.

Making money is a piece of the whole picture. You will also need to focus on keeping the business going. It is important that you always treat it as your business. What this means is you need to track your money, make smart decisions, and continue to learn as you go. This section will give you ideas on how to earn money and how to manage your business to grow something sustainable. You don't need a perfect plan to start. Begin with an idea and the willingness to take the first step. From there, build momentum and continue to move forward with consistency.

Money-Making Aspects of Business

- Sell products. Consider selling on social media platforms with ads or through Amazon, Shopify, or Etsy.
- Sell a service such as coaching, tutoring, freelancing, or courses.
- Sell a subscription for a podcast or a Patreon. People will pay for special notices, invites, videos, closed discussion groups, newsletters, and first-to-know updates.
- Earn money being an influencer. Get affiliate referrals, get advertisers, post on platforms, build a large following, and ask followers to help you go viral.

Learn These Important Aspects of Business

- Follow your money in and money out. Keep a spreadsheet or a record book.
- Keep your personal money and business money in different bank accounts.
- Be frugal when you start out. Spend only on what needs to be purchased at the moment. As your cash flow expands, you can decide on how much to allocate to things such as bookkeepers, staff, tax consultants, furniture, and so on. Eventually, you could have enough income to take a salary.
- Plan ahead for paying taxes; each state has different laws. Learn about state and federal tax laws (www.irs.gov/businesses, your state Department of Revenue, also called the tax commission or franchise tax board).
- Call your city or county to find out about obtaining a business license, business tax certificate, and if needed, a zoning permit. You can also get information from the Small Business Association (www.sba.gov/local-assistance).
- Attend industry events. Find groups of entrepreneurs on social media platforms. Join LinkedIn or Reddit groups. Talk to other business owners in your area. Learn from them.

Get support from others. Ask questions from other business owners. Everyone starts at the beginning. Start slowly, and get the word out about what you are doing. Join your local chamber of commerce to meet owners of businesses in your area.

Talk to many people, blast social media, get business cards, and have samples of products or designs stored on phone in a digital portfolio. Keep reminding yourself you can do this.

CHAPTER 15

Future Proofing for Personal Stability:
Mindsets for an Unpredictable World

Technology

As many of us have noticed, our world has rapidly moved forward in areas such as science, medical technology, and space exploration. One of the most controversial and exciting areas of development is artificial intelligence (AI).

AI is one of the fastest-growing areas of ingenuity in technology. Some people remain skeptical about its application, but AI is poised to grow swiftly in the next few years—and will affect everyone.

Not only can it shorten the time spent in many aspects of business, but AI can also help managers and HR departments screen résumés. It can be trained to utilize bias-reduction tools to have names ages and genders removed, and it can use chatbots for initial screening of job interview candidates. It can assist with scheduling and shift changes, and it is able to track sales information and help managers assess employee performance. It can recommend learning paths for employees and assist in answering questions related to basic protocol and important things for them to know.

AI presents many benefits for anyone willing to learn AI techniques, applications, and practice. With so many businesses interested in utilizing AI to streamline their workflow, training, and most other areas of running a business, this is a great area to get into as a career. A few respected companies train users within a matter of weeks or months depending on the depth of interest. Many colleges are now offering training programs in AI.

AI is already all around us, even if we don't always recognize it. It takes on different forms depending on the task.

AI learns from an enormous amount of data to make predictions and identify patterns. But not all AI works in the same way. For example, generative AI like ChatGPT can create new content, draft emails, write songs, make original images, or brainstorm with you. Smart assistants like Siri and Alexa are designed to respond to your voice commands, set reminders, answer quick questions, and connect with apps. Recommendation algorithms like the ones used on Spotify or Netflix learn what you like based on past choices and offer personalized selections for you to explore. AI can also recognize speech and images, automate tasks, translate languages, and help with everything from studying to producing business ideas. In all these forms, AI is becoming a powerful tool making tasks easier and more creative.

The possibilities seem endless.

But AI will not replace humans. Even the most advanced AI still depends on human input. It takes a cue to work for us by listening to our goals, creativity, and questions. It can process data and offer suggestions, but it doesn't understand context, emotions, and values. Humans still make the final decisions and choices. They use their judgment to shape how and what AI is used for. AI is a tool that acts as a powerful assistant; it helps you troubleshoot and improve how things run, but your ideas still lead the way.

In this day and age, it is imperative that you learn about AI. It is a swiftly moving industry that is growing week by week. Learn how it is used, and try out some of the infinite applications that are available. Keep up with it and have fun with it. I have explored creating artwork and music. I have searched for information and used it to create videos.

Personally, I find it fascinating, and the more I play around with it, the more my skills develop. AI is a tool. Explore and find out how using it can expand your knowledge and creativity. Here is a list of popular AI programs to explore:

- **ChatGPT (Open AI)** is a chatbot that can help you with writing, brainstorming, making outlines, answering questions, tutoring, getting information, and even getting recipes!
- **Midjourney** (an AI-powered graphic design tool) can generate high-quality digital art from text prompts.
- **Suno AI** (a music-generation tool) can generate original music and songs based on the user's input.
- **Runway** (a video editing and special effects tool) is used by filmmakers and content creators to create and enhance videos.

COVID Pandemic

We all went through the COVID-19 pandemic. It altered most things about life, including how we socialized, how we worked, and how we dealt with our health. Some people decided to get a covid vaccine, some people wore masks, distanced themselves from others and ceased visits to their medically vulnerable or elder family members. Others decided to take their chances and carry on as they normally would.

Many felt isolated during the pandemic, especially students when schools shut down. Stress levels rose and people worried about whether life would return to what it was.

2020 and 2021 saw the highest rates of death from the disease, especially among the elderly. In total, approximately 1.1 million people died in the United States alone according to statistics.

Many businesses closed temporarily. Over 330,000 work locations shut down permanently, and 1.2 million jobs were eliminated. Our country's gross domestic product dropped considerably due to factory shutdowns and business closures. Many businesses were able to recover by the start of 2023, but some are still feeling the sting of the pandemic's call for business closures.

During this horrifying period, people learned how to break their isolation by using different means to connect with others. People used Zoom and FaceTime to keep up with locals and those living far away. Some people used the time to take online courses, continue their studies, or take classes for enjoyment. Some people decided to challenge themselves to change their careers by learning new skills. Others sought accurate information to get a better understanding of what COVID-19 was. It was a perfect time for some to learn to cook, catch up on movies, or learn a language. Someone said to me when creating a series of childrens books, "I'm making lemonade out of a lemon of a terrible time."

Climate Change

Weather patterns have changed, with 2024 being the warmest year ever recorded. We have had extreme storms, record-breaking hot days, multiple tornadoes in one area, widespread drought, and fires that have scorched acres of land.

Climate change is happening. Greenhouse gas emissions have caused temperatures to rise. Many areas of the United States have experienced prolonged record-high temperatures.

Warming ocean temperatures have created stronger hurricanes and typhoons. When temperatures rise due to climate change, it enables the air to hold more moisture, which leads to heavier rainfall, causing a large increase in flooding incidents.

Wildfires brought on by drought and rising temperatures also affect air quality, often sending pollutants hundreds of miles away, creating unhealthy air for breathing. As these events become more commonplace, it is apparent that we must do something to change the course and heal the planet.

So what can you do? Here are some things that can be done to help with climate change:

- Walk, bike, or use public transportation.
- Compost plant-based foods. Eat a plant-based diet. Eat locally grown food. Plan meals and use leftovers.
- Avoid plastic products when you can.
- Plant trees. They help to absorb carbon dioxide and help to cool the planet by shading buildings and by releasing water vapor. They also prevent soil erosion.
- Plan your trips to do errands in one area at a time. This keeps you from driving all over, using more gas, and causing the release of more emissions.
- Use less energy. Unplug electronics when not in use, wash your clothes in cold water, and use LED lightbulbs.
- Purchase secondhand clothes, furniture, and sustainable products.

- Vote for leaders who support climate and environmental policies.
- Join a local environmental group, volunteer for park clean-up days, and remind people to follow fire alerts and not burn outdoors during fire seasons.

Politics

Over the past few years, politics have taken a very big turn. We have had a change in leadership different from what we have experienced in the last decade.

Having civil conversations about these changes is difficult at best. Where we will end up is anyone's guess.

For some, it has been hard to maneuver due to conflicting information. Many feel that ideologies have shifted our relationships with countries we previously had solid alliances with. Our country, at times, seems split between the old standards and emerging power dynamics between the three branches of government.

Get involved in local politics by supporting candidates who represent ideals similar to yours. Share ideas with others. Go to town hall meetings. Volunteer for campaigns or, when the time is right, run for office yourself.

You don't have to have the same ideas, but it is important to listen when discussing differences.

Education

Education has expanded from concentrating on degree-oriented learning to on-line-specific subject learning. Mastermind classes, summits, and course intensives allow you to focus on your area of interest and often allow for an in-depth learning experience over a shorter period of time.

Career and technical education include trades such as automotive repair, HVAC repair, carpentry, hospitality and tourism, and more. These types of programs offer focused study in shorter time frames than traditional four-year degree coursework.

The criteria may be changing to apply for grants, scholarships, and studying abroad. If this pertains to you, be sure to inquire early about what new requirements may be in effect.

Don't be afraid to further your learning. It can be more than just taking a class but also an opportunity to interact with people who have similar interests. It can help you to expand your circle and potentially meet people who can share their culture or talents. In a changing world, lifelong learning can keep you informed, expand your understanding of the world, and satisfy your curiosity.

Social Shifts

Our world is constantly fluctuating. Attitudes and beliefs change. What is important is knowing where you stand, recognizing that your perceptions may change over time. With constant shifts in culture, economics, politics, and social norms, change is a given. How you respond is what shapes your future.

Sometimes a mere conversation can open up a new means of seeing an issue or idea. Friendships, work experiences, education, and trying new things help to broaden your point of view.

You may have values that are steadfast and hold true to your identity. Whatever goes on around you, these core truths are the building blocks of how you live in the world. Questioning things, even if it's your own viewpoint, is perfectly fine to do. Being flexible can show a strength in character.

While some turns in your life may be scary, know that you can withstand shifts, and you can pursue goals. Oftentimes people find different ways to overcome difficult times by getting involved with their community, being engaged with others, and finding more satisfying ways to live.

Social Media

Social media continues to be a large factor for people who want to communicate with one another. Some use it to meet new people, while others use it to have discussions and keep abreast of current events and social issues.

Problems arise on social media, however, when the news is not portrayed accurately, when people make threats online, and when people try to take advantage of others. It can interfere with attempting to have a positive online experience.

If using the internet is upsetting to you, consider taking a break from social media. You can also alter how you use it. Set limits on time spent on the internet. Use it to learn something new; there are so many classes, workshops, and tutorials available. Instead of being on social media, have real conversations on Zoom or FaceTime with friends or family. Stay away from groups or subjects that help you lose confidence, feel depressed, or disconnected. Use social media as a tool to move to where you want to be by choosing something that uplifts you.

Things You Can Do to Adapt to Change

- Upgrade your skills throughout your life. Learning can take place through working with a mentor or coach or getting hands-on experience. Expand your scope by taking online courses and reading.
- Keep abreast of what is happening in the world. Follow reliable news sources, fact-check, and explore what is happening in fields like world news and politics. Keep up in the fields of medicine, science, and technology. Read about world history and world economics. This helps to put your own view into perspective with others' experiences.

- Find out about your own family history. If your grandparents are alive, interview them. Be sure to record it. Ask about where they grew up and what was happening at the different phases of their life (childhood, teens, college, work, marriage, etc.).
- Be flexible. Consider moving to areas in the country or abroad that you have not yet experienced. Try applying to new positions that you are qualified for but may not have thought of as an option for you. Be open to fewer workdays with longer hours.
- Some businesses like their employees to work remotely (usually from home). This can help to save on their overhead since they need less office space. This often can allow employees to manage their time differently than they might if they had a set time to be at work.

Critical Thinking

In this world that is frequently shifting with crises in climate change, unpredictable politics, rapid technological advances, and more, you can easily fall into an information conundrum (confusing or difficult problems).

Critical thinking is not only useful but it is essential. It helps you to bridge the gap between merely learning new skills and developing a mindset to navigate change, question what you hear, and make thoughtful decisions when the path may not be clear. Whether you are attempting to filter through false news, trying to make a decision about investing money in an unstable market, or exploring how AI can improve your life, critical thinking can help you to adapt. It also helps you to make the best choices while staying true to your values, goals, and understanding of how the world works.

Develop your ability for critical thinking by using the following steps:

- Understand the key elements of the information received.
- Learn to assess the credibility of the information read.
- Examine evidence on a subject or situation before coming to a conclusion.

- Use logical thinking when problem-solving.
- Be open to new ideas and different perspectives.
- Understand your own thought process. Know when you have a bias that may interfere with developing an accurate picture of what is going on.
- Examine both sides of an argument before you come to a conclusion.

As our world becomes more complex it is important to fact-check news before sharing it. Beware of online misinformation. Do not sit listening to the news for many hours. Many people have experienced depression, anxiety, anger, and fear during shaky times.

Other Ways to Have a Full Life During Difficult Times

- Have a strong network of friends, family, peers, mentors, and teachers to discuss important aspects of life. Seek support when difficult topics arise or you are working to achieve something new.
- If needed, receive counseling so you can focus on your issues. This can help you to deal with and control anxiety, sadness, depression, anger, or any other feelings and issues that arise.
- Try to eat healthy foods, get enough sleep, and exercise. Focus on well-being when the world seems chaotic.
- Develop ways to cope with stress. Look to recreation with friends, playing an instrument, reading, being creative, taking a walk, walking your dog, or whatever helps you feel grounded or relaxed or takes your mind off upsetting circumstances.
- Don't forget it's OK to have fun. This can help to ward off a doom-and-gloom mentality.
- Do things that you enjoy, such as cooking and having people over. Go to events. Some people attend rallies and feel good being part of a larger community of people with a similar mindset.

- Find solace and comfort, whether through breathwork and meditation, biking, reading a book on the patio, or anything else that helps you focus.

Keep your eye on what is happening in the world and pay attention to what you might accomplish during this period of transition.

CHAPTER 16

The End is The Beginning

This book is the culmination of my lessons, experiences, and information gained. I started out with the idea a number of years ago. It is now completed, giving me a sense of fulfillment, satisfaction, and hope that young adults can live their lives with confidence and meaning.

The experiences we have create substance in life. Some may be difficult or painful; some bring us joy and understanding. We get through life despite things. We have stories to tell. Sometimes we have dragons to slay. We go through the springs and winters and discover we are yet again survivors in life. We have another go at it. It's knowing that cycle, that there is more. It whispers, "Try again, continue."

It takes courage to begin and proceed with this exploration. You now have tools to tackle some of life's issues. Maybe you will attempt a new relationship or go on a solo trip somewhere you have never ventured to before. Possibly you will have more fluid conversations with family members and develop closer relationships. Maybe you will start your own business or work on an issue that gets in your way with a therapist.

Now it is time to set off on your own journey forward. You do not have to have a complete roadmap; you will mark your path as you venture into the world. Save room to make mistakes and experience surprises. Perfection is overrated—it's OK to change your mind! Now you are prepared to make choices for yourself—think critically. You get to design your life. How incredible is that?

I thank you for joining me on this adventure. Be true to who you know you are. May your road be varied. Stay resilient and take on new challenges with confidence. May you have many adventures!

Resources

Food

"The Blue Zones Kitchen" by Dan Buettner; *National Geographic*, 2019; Photographs by David McLain.

"The Blue Zones Challenge" by Dan Buettner; *National Geographic*, 2021.

The Food Revolution: How Your Diet Can Help Save Your Life and Our World by John Robbins; Conari Press, 2011.

Real Superfoods: Everyday Ingredients to Elevate Your Health by Ocean Robbins and Nichole Dandrea-Russet; Food Revolution Network, 2023.

The Complete Plant-Based Cookbook; America's Test Kitchen, 2020.

Farm to Fork: Cooking Local, Cooking Fresh by Emeril Lagasse; Harper Collins Publishers, 2010.

The Complete Spanish Cookbook by Pepita Aris; Arness Publishing LTD, 2012.

The Complete Middle East Cookbook by Tess Mallos; Tuttle Publishing, 2007.

The Body, Health, Mental Health, and Fitness

National Institute of Health (NIH); https://nih.gov/.

Your Healthiest Self: Physical Wellness Toolkit; National Institute of Health, 2025. https://www.nih.gov/health-information/your-healthiest-self-wellness-toolkits/.

The Body Keeps the Score: Brain, Mind, Body in the Healing of Trauma by Bessel van der Kolk; Penguin Books, 2015.

Spark: The Revolutionary New Science of Exercise and the Brain by Dr. John J. Rafey and Eric Hagerman; Little, Brown, Spark, 2013.

Protect Your Peace: Nine Unapologetic Principles for Thriving in a Chaotic World by Trent Shelton; Hay House Inc., 2024.

Finances and Entrepreneurship

Rework by Jason Fried; Crown Currency, 2010.

Start Something That Matters by Blake Mycoskie; Virgin Publishing, 2012.

Unshakable: Your Financial Freedom Playbook by Tony Robbins; Simon and Shuster, 2018.

Millionaire Success Habits: The Gateway to Wealth and Prosperity by Dean Graziosi; Hay House Business, 2023.

The Little Book of Common Sense Investing by John C. Bogle; Wiley, 2017.

The Oracle Speaks: Warren Buffet in His Own Words by David Andrews; Agate B2, 2012.

Politics/Government

A Users Guide to Democracy: How America Works by Nick Capodice and Hannah McCarthy; Celadon Books, 2020.

Politics Is for Power by Eitan Hersh; Scribner, 2020.

Why We Are Polarized by Ezra Klien; Avid Reader Press, 2021.

The Constitution of the United States of America; East India Publishing Company, 2020.

Personal Growth

Critical Thinking: A Comprehensive Beginner's Guide to Rational Analysis and Creative Problem Solving by Kevin Brown; 2024

Atomic Habits: Tiny Changes, Remarkable Results by James Clear; Avery Publishing, 2018.

Creativity

The Work of Art: How Something Comes From Nothing by Adam Moss; Penguin Press, 2024.

Basic Art: Dali by Gilles Neret; Taschen American LLC., 2015.

How Music Works by David Byrne; Crown, 2017.

How to Sing Without Thinking by Gabriel Weiner; Cuerpo y Alma, 2024.

Gaudí: The Complete Works by Rainer Zerbst; Taschen America LLC., 2020.

Leave a review

for *The Life Guide You Actually Need*, sign up for Lisa's newsletter, and follow on social media by scanning the QR code or going to the URL below:

https://linktr.ee/l.piatetsky.author

www.ingramcontent.com/pod-product-compliance
Lightning Source LLC
Chambersburg PA
CBHW081358290426
44110CB00018B/2407